W9-BSF-304

# *The*

# SUCCESS

# TOOLBOX

## *for*

# ENTREPRENEURS

# *The* SUCCESS TOOLBOX

## *for* ENTREPRENEURS

## Janis Vos

LIFESUCCESS PUBLISHING, LLC
8900 E Pinnacle Peak Road, Suite D240
Scottsdale, AZ 85255

| | |
|---|---|
| Telephone: | 800.473.7134 |
| Fax: | 480.661.1014 |
| E-mail: | admin@lifesuccesspublishing.com |
| ISBN: | 978-1-59930-005-4 |
| Cover : | LifeSuccess Publishing, LLC |
| Layout: | LifeSuccess Publishing, LLC |

COMPANIES, ORGANIZATIONS, INSTITUTIONS, AND INDUSTRY PUBLICATIONS: Quantity discounts are available on bulk purchases of this book for reselling, educational purposes, subscription incentives, gifts, sponsorship, or fundraising. Special books or book excerpts can also be created to fit specific needs such as private labeling with your logo on the cover and a message from a VIP printed inside. For more information, please contact our Special Sales Department at LifeSuccess Publishing, LLC.

# DEDICATION

This book is dedicated to my friend, my husband, and my success partner in life – Curt. He has encouraged and supported me in my quest to publish this book, and I love him for that. I thank you, dear Curt, for your love and support.

# PRAISE FOR

## *The Success Toolbox for Entrepreneurs*

*"As a retired executive of a large corporation, I realize that what Janis has described in her book is what I needed long ago to free myself of the corporate maze. The perks it offers sucks one into its web, which is not always in tune with one's own best interests. Today I have the privilege of working with Janis through our Mastermind calls , and I am applying her S's in a new business venture at the ripe young age of seventy-seven. This book will help you decide and empower you to pursue the path toward fulfilling your dreams and aspirations."*

**- Bob Childs, retired engineering executive**

*"This book and the nine S's helped me to quickly and clearly put my business venture into action. Janis helped me to develop every piece of the puzzle and to have the confidence to move forward to financial and personal freedom."*

**- Lisa Rigato, president Daystar Visions Inc**.

*"This is a must-read for entrepreneurs. It will show you how to build a profitable business venture using a hands-on, practical approach."*

**– Gerry Robert, bestselling author of**
*The Millionaire Mindset*

**"** *The Success Toolbox for Entrepreneurs really made me realize how important systems are for your business success. As an entrepreneur who has turned real estate into a profitable venture, I now know how to increase my results."*

**– Jason Childs, real estate broker and investor**

*"Janis Vos is one of the most influential powerhouses of success I know. She has helped me focus on prosperity and has been a magnificent part of the persistence it takes to get you where you want to go… 'Enjoy the Ride'…"*

**– Colin Markin, LifeSuccess Mastermind**
**101 Facilitator/life coach**

# CONTENTS

FOREWORD                                    11

ACKNOWLEDGEMENTS                            13

KNOWING WHERE YOU ARE                       17

IMAGINING                                   35

GETTING STARTED                             49

FIRST S - STRATEGY                          53

BUILDING THE RIGHT STRUCTURE                71

SKILLS                                      81

SYSTEMS                                     101

SOCIAL                                      111

SENSE                                       119

SPIRIT                                      127

SUCCESS                                     147

SHARING                                     163

# FOREWORD

## *The Success Toolbox for Entrepreneurs*

This is it! This is the book that will help you explore your entrepreneurial spirit. Not only does Janis encourage you to have the courage to explore, she gives you the tools required to implement business strategies in anything you attempt.

It may be investing in a new business venture, inventing something new, already owning a business, buying a franchise, or you may be building a network marketing company. Whatever your dream is, Janis will help you to realize it.

*The Success Toolbox for Entrepreneurs* does this by offering you some critical key elements – the nine S's – that give you the tools that you or others working with you need to succeed.

Janis takes it further by defining the need for BALANCE in work and personal lifestyle.

In each chapter, she gives you a description of each S and then some examples and ideas to help you along as you build yourself and your business venture to success. She recommends books and resources that have influenced her thinking and results that will be of assistance to you as you build your dream. Her website will link you to ideas that you can implement immediately.

I highly recommend this book and ask you to enjoy your entrepreneurial journey!

**Gerry Robert, bestselling author of**
*The Millionaire Mindset*

# ACKNOWLEDGEMENTS

There are so many people who have come into my life over the last six years who have significantly influenced my path and my success. Because of them I have realized my purpose in life is to commit to life-long learning and to inspire others to learn through my words, stories, beliefs, and enthusiasm.

The following people have significantly influenced me, and I want to thank them and to share with you a little bit about each of them.

Bob Proctor came into my life through a network marketing company that had the foresight to invite Bob and his colleague, John Kanary, to Alberta. This series of events led me to become a student of Bob Proctor and subsequently to become a LifeSuccess Coach, teaching the principles that Bob Proctor has spent his life teaching.

Gerry Robert is the author of the bestselling *The Millionaire Mindset* and the owner of LifeSuccess Publishing. His revolutionary approach to attracting customers through publishing books really turned me on. Having the privilege to work with Gerry in Alberta to show others how a book can change your marketing approach forever was an exciting opportunity in my life. It has been his generosity and encouragement that has helped me get this book done.

Carol Gates, of LifeSuccess Productions, is someone that I greatly admire because of her dedication and loyalty to the LifeSuccess coaches and because of her book, *As You Wish*, which inspired me to realize I could achieve the same success with my book.

Because of the wonderful people above, I have met extraordinary people along my journey with Bob Proctor and his team. You know who you are, and I am so truly grateful to have been a part of your lives.

Let me introduce my Mastermind members: Lisa Rigato, Teri Rigato, Jason Childs, Bob Childs, Lisa Czarnecki, and Ines Rivas. These are the wonderful people who over the past three years have supported me and loved me. I am truly grateful to have them as friends and business developers as we realize great success together. Our study of Napoleon Hill's *Think and Grow Rich* has forever changed our lives, and I include this wonderful man's spirit in our Mastermind success.

Ray Guidinger walked into one of my leadership classes at Acklands Grainger. From the minute he walked into the room, I knew we would be friends, and I have had the privilege of working with him on many projects. I have been able to round out my book because of those experiences.

Colin Markin is a LifeSuccess Consultant and a wonderful friend. We have traveled together as LifeSuccess coaches, following Bob Proctor across the United States. Colin and I have implemented these ideas in both Alberta and British Columbia, and I look forward to a life of creating with Colin.

Glen Hommy is my friend, business partner and mentor. He supported this book financially and gave me his time and encouragement so that you could read about his entrepreneurial journey and be inspired to do the same.

Bruce Kirkland shared his time and story with me so I could bring to you real examples of how this book works.

Last but not least, I want to acknowledge the writers and the creators of ideas who have so inspired me and changed me as a person. They are Dr. Wayne Dyer, Esther and Jerry Hicks, Earl Nightingale, Joe Vitale, James Allen, Robert Kiyosaki, Bob Doyle, Price Pritchett, John Kalench, James Ferriss and Raymond Holliwell.

Thank you all for the inspiration and joy you have brought to me and your influence that has contributed to the creation of this book.

- Janis

# CHAPTER

---

## KNOWING WHERE YOU ARE

My father was a tool- and die-maker and a master carpenter. He always had toolboxes in our home, and one in particular stands out for me. He made it from oak, and it had six drawers in the front where my dad had his specialty tools carefully placed. The tools were organized in a precise system that allowed my dad to always find the tool he needed for the job at hand. I still have that toolbox in my living room to remind me of how precious the organized tools were to him and how we all need tools to guide us in our business and personal lives. This book is designed like my dad's toolbox. It is organized in a step-by-step manner, following nine S's that will help you to identify where you are as an entrepreneur, to prosper, and to balance your life as you receive the results you truly desire.

My dad was an entrepreneur. At the age of fifty-five he left a large company with a pension to start Ithaca Gun Company of Canada. He did not know about guns, but he had a dream; he knew how to run the company, and his move allowed our family to prosper. His journey showed me that you can learn anything as long as you have the passion to make it happen.

In order to succeed as an entrepreneur you must acknowledge where you are and then know **WHERE YOU WANT TO BE.** This book explores nine key S's and gives you tools that will help you to identify and understand your present results and then to set a course for the future.

Why did I write this book? Over my many years of listening to people within and without companies express their discontent, frustration, and anger, I realized they needed something to help them create a new path for themselves.

Spending twenty years buried within companies as an entrepreneur affected my spirit until I began to realize I could set a True North course for myself and uncover my entrepreneurial spirit and achieve success.

# SETTING YOUR TRUE NORTH COURSE

What do I mean by True North? Well, let me share with you my idea of True North. A true Canadian symbol that represents my True North is the Inukshuk (pronounced IN-OOK-SHOOK), meaning "in the image of man."

Sculpture by Zazo

*"The Inukshuks are magnificent lifelike figures of stone which were erected by the Inuit people and are unique to the Canadian Arctic. They were erected to make the way easier for those who follow, and the Inukshuk represents safety and nourishment, trust and reassurance. The Inukshuk guided people across the frozen tundra and gave them hope in barren places to handle hardships they encountered." (www.sulis.net)*

This symbol is my True North. It guides me safely down my life's path, and it encourages me to reach my goals and attain my vision. It points me in an outward direction to take risks, to take chances, and it is always there for me when I need to come back. It is my marker and a safety valve. It is also a symbol of our human spirit, teaching us the ability to succeed with others, where alone we would fail.

This is the necklace I wear with these symbols. The Inukshuk focuses me on where I dare to go, and the diamond shines brightly, promising me success.

What is your True North? Think about what is important to you as I help you to imagine your business venture and your life. Along this journey there will be a symbol that becomes meaningful to you. I will also help you to explore your purpose in life; let it lead you to your entrepreneurial True North.

*"If you fail to determine your definite purpose, everything else is wrong. It's like working with a broken compass — you may think you're going North, but you're not. You're not sure which direction you're heading, so you're just wandering aimlessly.*

*Without your purpose identified firmly in your mind, you will wander through life, never quite feeling that you're in the flow. I say, then, it's imperative that you recognize what it is you're good at — what it is you really love to do. Your purpose in this lifetime is to do the thing that you love."*

**- Bob Proctor**

# WHAT IS AN ENTREPRENEUR?

As an entrepreneur, you may be investing in a new business venture, inventing something new, already owning a business, buying a franchise, or you may be building a business through network marketing. Whatever the case, you need to clearly understand where you are before you move to what you really want.

*Entrepreneur (plural entrepreneurs)*

Definition from Wiktionary

1.  A person who takes the risk of turning an opportunity into profit.

2. A person who takes the risk of managing and operating a business or businesses; term often used:

a. for one who does this for one or more businesses that he or she entirely or largely helps to create;

b. for one who takes on ownership, or significant ownership, of one or more business franchises.

3. A person who is talented or prolific at developing new programs inside existing organizations.

Why have I given you three definitions? Because there are people who are entrepreneurs who don't even know that they are. I spent my entire career developing new programs, processes, and ideas and saving hundreds of thousands of dollars inside the companies I worked for. Now I do it for myself.

# TODAY'S EMPLOYMENT SYSTEMS EQUAL SLAVERY

*"In North America today there appear to be two systems of employment. One is voluntary and the other one is organized; however, **both could be called slavery.**"*

**- Dr. Curt Vos**

Permit me to explain. There are people every day voluntarily putting in extra time for someone else's business and not being rewarded for it. They are career people who continue to work harder and harder to prove their worth. These people go to work early and stay late to get caught up. They take on more and more responsibility without an increase in pay. They are given a computer from the company and use it at home, on the plane, and in the hotel room at all times of the day and night. Cell phones have linked them to the world, but they have taken over every spare minute of their time.

There are others who are working for the **organized** corporate world and never being paid what they are worth. These people see no way out and are in bondage in their minds to the company. Because of their thinking, they are unable to see a future on their own. They are slaves because they worry about losing their jobs or because they are bound to a pension they will receive at the end of thirty years. Some of these people have been taught by their parents that if you get a job and put in hard, extra work, you will be rewarded.

*It is time to step out of your box and realize that there are options. This book will help give you not only courage, but a model to follow for success.*

Yes, there are people who are born entrepreneurs, and you are going to meet some of them in this book and hear their stories. But don't discount yourself if it doesn't come as naturally as you think it should. You can learn to become an entrepreneur, and this book will assist you in realizing your dream.

This book shares some of my stories, not to brag, but to share with you stories with which you can identify, and to inspire you to consider where you are right now and where you truly want to go. It guides you through nine key tools and it will give you examples of what works. It will continue to stretch you to visualize what you really want your business venture to become. Then we will concentrate on what your personal life looks like in conjunction with your success.

Building the business team and attracting the investors, not working in the business, is the principle that I apply when I am moving into a new business. Today we need to work smarter, not harder. I have been influenced by Robert Kiyosaki, author of *Rich Dad Poor Dad*, who truly understands entrepreneurship and how to educate people to become better investors. Playing his Cashflow game for the first time caused me nothing but frustration. I could not get out of the rat race, while my husband, Curt, seemed to effortlessly get out and succeed. On the second try, however, I was determined to get it, and I was out in no time and started to realize what it takes to get onto the fast track.

It has taken me a long time to get this. When I was downsized from my corporate job in 1996, I decided that I would not work for anyone else again. So I started my own company, JAK & Company Ltd., consulting as a business specialist to many companies, showing them how to implement systems and building business plans that would move them into the future.

I also became a training consultant to several companies operating in western Canada.

I soon realized that I did not have the control I needed. I was still at the beck and call of my clients and not getting the results I wanted. What I should have understood is that, as Robert Kiyosaki points out, I was still trading time for money, and it was at the whim of a company when I was paid.

However, during this period I started to realize that the process I was applying was a combination of skills that I had learned from some of the consultants who had been hired in my previous business positions and of concepts that I had created that could move an entrepreneur more quickly to success.

This is exactly what I started to do. I applied what I knew to my own entrepreneurial spirit and I took control of my own destiny.

Now enough about me, let's get back to you!

Where are you in your business life? Are you in a job you hate and know you should be breaking free from and taking the risk to success? As an entrepreneur, you must look at where you are and then determine the results you want – if results are what you want! What do you want? Have a clear goal in mind. Make it so big that it scares and excites you at the same time.

# MULTIPLE STREAMS OF INCOME (MSI)

My mentor and personal coach, Bob Proctor, often talks about Multiple Streams of Income, or MSIs. He explains three strategies that people use when accumulating wealth:

**Strategy one** is used by 96 percent of the population, and it is the worst strategy that you can use. It is trading time for money – in other words, a job where you only have so much time to make so much money, and if you save any money it is at the expense of a life. That is not balance, and it takes a toll every time.

**Strategy two** is when you use your money to make money, often through investments, such as the stock market or real estate. About three percent of the population apply this strategy and have a successful outcome.

**Strategy three** is the most effective – yet only one percent of the population use it. This is when you multiply your time by having multiple streams of revenue. This is the strategy you want to develop, and yet so many people are afraid or don't know how to go about this.

How would you like to be among the four percent of those who know how to create wealth? Strategy three, of course, is where you want to be, multiplying your time through multiple streams of revenue. As Bob Proctor says, never let the postman go by your door without leaving a cheque behind. This is where you need to put your effort, and yet only one percent of the population do this and receive 96 percent of the reward. Why?

Bob Proctor has spent his life encouraging people to build Multiple Streams of Income (MSIs). Through his seminar, *The Science of Getting Rich*, he has helped my husband Curt and I to understand what it takes to not only build Multiple Streams of Income but how to attract wealth quickly.

We have a Multiple Streams of Income wheel that we redraw every year. It shows us in the middle doing what we truly love, and all around the center-circle we have mapped out investments, businesses, creative ideas, inventions, money flow, and assets. This keeps us on track and helps us to realize from where and how the next cash flow is coming.

## MULTIPLE STREAMS OF INCOME WHEEL

Some examples of building multiple sources of income include:

1. Owning a business and letting someone else run it

2. Franchise

3. Inventing

4. Royalty cheques

5. Network marketing

6. Investments

7. Licensing

8. Stocks

9. Pensions

10. Rental Properties

11. Real Estate

12. Internet

13. Alliances with others

Owning your own business can be profitable if you apply the principles you find in this book. Again, there is usually a large investment up front in order to get started; however, if your idea is sound you will always attract investors. One business owner I talked with, when I asked him if he was the owner, stated that it depended on what I meant. He went on to explain that actually, the TD Bank owned his business, and he was basically working the business to get out from under the debt load.

The advantage of owning a franchise is that the system is already in place for you, and you strictly follow what has proved to be successful in the past. Lots of money can be made here. However, there is a large investment up front to purchase the franchise, and you may not see any profits for two to three years. You are very involved on a daily basis to ensure the success of the venture.

Inventing a new process, product, or service; now this is where the creative juices can flow. There may be a large investment upfront, or you will need to attract people willing to invest in your idea. The key here is to know where to find the specialized knowledge to help you move your idea to market. Having a sound business plan, understanding business stewardship, and being able to take your idea to market are the keys.

Finding investors to help you get started as an entrepreneur is critical. One site that I have found that seems complete and truly keeps it simple is www.go4funding.com. Their platform is to bring entrepreneurs and investors closer together. Find someone who appeals to you to help move you forward.

Think royalties. To create a steady stream of income for yourself, create new ideas and spin them off to others who are willing to take your ideas and fly with them. The game of Monopoly is a great example of how this can be accomplished.

One of the ways to build Multiple Streams of Income is in direct selling or network marketing. Network marketing companies have some of the most sophisticated systems in the world. They are heralding in the new economy using the Internet and showing ordinary people how to create extraordinary income.

Building a solid business team is one way to focus your attention on taking a network marketing business to the top. Indeed, today more and more companies are realizing the benefits of taking their business into direct sales. There is no huge infrastructure; people are consultants to the company, not employees; and they are working from home, building a team, and focusing on their own success and thus the success of the company. It is a team spirit that encourages creativity, not competition. However, you must have desire and faith, and you must believe in what you are doing. If you enter a network marketing business thinking you can make a lot of money overnight, you are kidding yourself. There is hard work involved and a learning curve that you will need others to help you with. However, the benefits include working from home, part time or full time, and you are in control of your destiny.

Investments have been one of the main systems that have been encouraged by the large financial institutions and brokers. This can include stocks and bonds, real estate, and blue chip stocks. In past years, some of these investments have not done too well, but they do represent security to some people. This book is not going into this subject; however, you should find someone you trust to give you advice on these investments.

Some people, as they read this, will know that they will receive a pension at the end of their career with a company. Some pensions will be significant and others will not. They can still be considered a Multiple Stream of Income that it is great to know you will have to add to your repertoire of income.

The Internet has become the market of choice for creating wealth. Learning to become creative through an internet opportunity can be a significant contributor to your wheel of income. Creating alliances with other sites such as Amazon,

E-Bay, or Bob Proctor's LifeSuccess Productions can bring you a steady stream of income. This, combined with the ideas above, will start to create Multiple Streams of Income.

This book is part of my MSI wheel from a perspective of selling the book, giving it away as a marketing tool, and then attracting people to me who want my expertise as a speaker and facilitator.

## MOVING FORWARD

No matter where you are as an entrepreneur, this book will help you realize what you need to be successful. Even if you have never had the courage to step out and try, this book will give you practical steps to follow to guide you to success.

The choices that you make will allow you to grow your dream without having to put your own life out of balance to achieve results.

If you look at the past method of making money for the majority of people, it has included working for a corporation, doing a good job, putting in lots of extra hours, hopefully getting recognized, and progressing in the company with some monetary compensation. Oh, and maybe there will be a pension and maybe there won't. I did this for more than 30 years. This is part of the system I talked about at the beginning of this book.

What course have you set for your business and personal life? This book will help you to decide, to plan, and to consider nine

S's that will allow you to make the right decisions early on to ensure that your business life is working the way I know it can.

Some of you reading this are saying, "Oh, sure, leave my job and the security it brings me." I am not saying you have to leave your job. I am saying that you need to start to dream about what you truly want and then practice putting these tools into place to set you up for an amazing future when you are ready.

Some of you may decide to leave your job. It does take courage to allow your entrepreneurial spirit to soar, and it takes a plan. This book will help you to develop that plan in nine key areas; then you have to have the courage and faith to take a step out.

As you read through this book, you may need to gather other tools from another direction. The resources that I give you will identify ideas that will resonate with you. You are starting to gather the tools and the organization of the toolbox to give you success for the future.

Identify your True North and move toward it.

*"When you reach an obstacle, turn it into an opportunity. You have the choice. You can overcome and be a winner, or you can allow it to overcome you and be a loser. The choice is yours and yours alone. Refuse to throw in the towel. Go that extra mile that failures refuse to travel. It is far better to be exhausted from success than to be rested from failure."*

**-Mary Kay Ash, founder of Mary Kay Cosmetics**

*"I never perfected an invention that I did not think about in terms of the service it might give others: find out what the world needs then I proceed to invent."*

**-Thomas Edison**

*"The important thing is not being afraid to take a chance. Remember, the greatest failure is not to try. Once you find something you love to do, be the best at doing it."*

**-Debbi Fields, founder of Mrs. Fields Cookies**

*"Our success has really been based on partnerships from the very beginning."*

**-Bill Gates**

# CHAPTER

## IMAGINING

## IMAGINING YOUR PERFECT BUSINESS VENTURE

In the foreword to *The Science of Getting Rich*, Bob Proctor talks about his rich relationship with Lloyd Connant. Bob relates moments in time when Lloyd would raise his hand above his head as if it were reaching into the heavens, and he would close his eyes and lead Bob and his colleague to imagine how their company would look. Lloyd called this *Imagineering*.

I am going to take you on the journey with me to imagine what YOU want. What do you want, what do you really want? This was one of the hardest exercises I have ever had to think about. One of the programs I coach, *The Goal Achiever*, asks you to list thirty things that you want. When I was asked to do this under Bob Proctor's coaching program, I couldn't even think of five. How foolish of me. Once I started to use my imagination, the whole world opened up and I listed 30 easily. As a matter of fact, looking back at that list of two years ago, I have achieved most of them.

## WHERE HAS YOUR CHILD GONE?

As children, we have incredible imagination. We can dream, visualize, and imagine anything we want. In my early years, I ran around our neighborhood, neighing like a horse or barking like a dog, really believing I was one – and I have pictures to prove it.

I was sure I could fly; I had vivid dreams every night about flying over fences, not too far off the ground, but I knew I could. I spent my youth bruised because I kept trying to fly and ended up falling out of trees, off porches, fences, and anywhere I was sure I could get a good leap into the air.

Where does the ability to imagine go as we grow up? We are encouraged to stop imagining and focus on what the schools are telling us, what our adult friends are telling us, and yes, even what our parents are telling us; to grow up and stop dreaming.

Well, I am telling you that you have to DREAM! Dream bigger than you have ever dreamed! Let me share a secret with you. I never bought into this notion of not dreaming because I was a grown up. I still neigh like a horse and bark like a dog, and I have spent my last 25 years playing a clown for children. I kept my inner child despite all those people who would have robbed me of it. I know how to dream and to experience joy.

Come with me and imagine. Imagine what you want your business life to be like, how much money you want to make, how happy you want to be, and how healthy you want to feel. What balance will you have between your personal and business life?

You can have it all, and I am going to help you to look in detail at the business life you truly want to build and to ensure its success.

Start by visualizing and creating a fantasy of what you want. Really imagine: if there were nothing in your way, what would you want your entrepreneurial venture to look like? If you could paint a picture or describe the picture to someone else, what would it look like? What would it be like to work there? How would others treat one another? How many people are you working with, and what kind of money would the business and you be making? Do you have partners? Are you in creation mode rather than competition mode? Are you investing in or creating new products?

Detail is the key, as much as you can possibly add, even the way things smell and taste – all your senses should be inspired to dream and create the vision you want.

Walk through in your mind what it would feel like to live in your business venture. Where is it located? How does it feel to be there? What kind of people have you surrounded yourself with? Are you alone and enjoying every minute of it? Are you building an entire team with values the same as yours? Are you creating and feeling the synergy between you and others?

Really concentrate on the business you want. Close your eyes and feel yourself there. Write down all the things that are important to you about the business you are visualizing. Write it down. The moment the ideas are on paper your dream will start to take shape.

I believe in flip-chart paper, and 3M helped me become even better at it when they invented the chart paper with the sticky backing that hangs on anything and does not bleed through to the wall. My office is filled with 3M flip-chart paper and with ideas. Goals, visions, and dreams are all arranged, taking me forward to the future.

Take some serious time to decide what you want and then move forward in this book to understand. Once you have the picture, the dream, and the vision, this book can help you realize how to ensure that it happens. If you are having trouble doing this, find pictures that represent what you want. Cut them out and paste them all around you. This will inspire you to start to create and imagine the perfect business.

On the next page, put down specific details of what you want and what you imagine in your mind. If you need to cut out pictures of what your business venture is going to look like, do it. Now get emotionally involved with this picture. What will it feel like to be in this business? When you walk through it, what do you see and feel? Really concentrate on these feelings and the results you want from your enterprise. Use your five senses to bring the vision to life.

The importance of this exercise comes from the Law of Attraction. We attract what we think about. We will explore this law throughout the book. By visualizing and feeling what you really want in your entrepreneurial quest, you will begin to attract everything you need to succeed.

# VISUALIZATION EXERCISE

To visualize is defined by the Encarta dictionary as "create positive mental picture of something." A key part of the visualization process is the ability to meditate and concentrate on a picture of what you want in your business and life.

Both Lisa Czarnecki and Ines Rivas are on our Mastermind calls on Sundays. In my opinion both of them truly understand meditation and how to create the picture you want for yourself.

Ines is a successful real estate agent in San Antonio, Texas. She claims that you need to start off as simply as possible when you are meditating. Here are her recommendations:

*"I have been using Transcendental Meditation for about 25 years; it has been very helpful to the mind, the body, relationships, in every area of my life. What I do is this: I sit comfortably in a very quiet place in the morning when I get up. I inhale*

*and exhale (consciously doing this at least 20 times). Then I concentrate on breathing in and out for a few minutes, relax and let the mind wander, with the eyes closed. I do not think of anything specific; I free my mind.*

*"By doing this exercise twice a day × 20 minutes, in the morning and at night before going to bed, I get a deep rest and recharge the energy in my body. After this exercise I feel great, rested as new! One of the most important things is to make it a habit to do it twice a day EVERY DAY. Practice, practice, practice — the more you do it, the better you get at meditation."*

**Lisa has shared a script that she uses every day as she meditates:**

## A GUIDED MEDITATION BY LISA CZARNECKI

"To start to relax, find a private place where you will not be interrupted by any disruptions or noise. Remove your tight-fitting clothes, eyeglasses and jewelry.

"Sit with your back straight.

"Concentrate on your breathing

"Inhale deeply into the bottom of your lungs for a count of 3 – 1 2 3

"Now exhale slowly for a count of 3 – 1 2 3

"Inhale slowly for the count of 4 – 1 2 3 4

"Exhale slowly for a count of 4 – 1 2 3 4

"Slow it down again for the count of 5 – 1 2 3 4 5

"Exhale slowly for the count of 5 – 1 2 3 4 5

"Step by step, slow your breathing down to a level that your own body will allow.

*"On your own, find the level that is the most comfortable for you.*

"Wait about 3 minutes…

"I am going to count downward from 10 to zero… feel yourself becoming more relaxed with every number counted… so calm, comfortable, relaxed.

(10) Think of the muscles in your scalp and forehead growing very comfortable and relaxed… you will find that as you think of these muscles they will start to relax.

Feel the tiny muscles of the eyelids relax… let the relaxation move deep inside the eyes and deep in the back of the eyes.

(9) Let all the facial muscles relax… cheekbones and the cheeks… jaw and chin… lips and mouth relax…

Let the relaxation move deep inside your mouth as the muscles of the mouth relax… you find that your mouth automatically becomes not too dry and not too moist, just enough to keep it moist enough to keep you perfectly comfortable.

(8) Feel the relaxation spread deep into the back of the throat… deep into the back of the head and neck … deep into the neck and shoulders.

(7) Now let the arms relax… relax the upper arms… concentrate on the forearms and feel them relax… all the muscles between the elbow and the wrist… feel the relaxation spreading across the top of the hands and deep into the hands… across the palms and deep into the palms and into your finger tips. Deep through the hands… now the fingers… relax all the way to the fingertips…

(6) Bring your attention back again to the relaxed muscles of the neck and shoulders… let the relaxation flow into the chest and lungs… your breathing is easy and gentle… and you feel yourself relaxing more and more with each gentle breath. You're relaxed more and more into each easy breath.

(5) Feel the relaxation further down into the broad of the back. Feel the relaxation move down your spine into the small of your back. Feel the relaxation spreading around and deep into the sides… let the muscles of the abdomen relax deep into the abdomen. All the muscles of the abdomen and hips relax.

(4) Now let the legs relax… feel the relaxation spreading into the thighs and knees… the calves relax all the way to the ankle. Now let the feet relax, the heel, the underside, deep through the feet to the tops, and finally even the toes relax.

(3) It feels so good to relax and let go of all tension and all care.

(2) As I continue to talk now, nothing more than the sound of my voice helps lure you into a very restful and relaxing form of sleep. All worldly things seem very remote now as you go down into the most restful sleep that you have ever known and could possibly imagine… a wonderful, warm, restful, peaceful sleep… a dreamless sleep

(1) Almost to the bottom now, and you are completely relaxed.

All muscular tension and all emotional tension is gone; all mental tension is disappearing now, and with the next number you will enter a beautiful, restful, and peaceful, serene place where there is nothing to do, no one to bother you, nothing to disturb you, no one you have to please, no one you have to satisfy… there is only physical and emotional peace, comfort, and tranquility.

*"Are you ready to enter this beautiful place now?*

"Wonderful.

"And now zero:

"Relax more deeply than you have ever known yourself to be. As you go deeper... deeper and deeper into this sleep state... so calm, so comfortable... so relaxed... with each gentle and easy breath you take, with every minute that passes... with each and every word I speak to you, just relax even more and go deeper and deeper to sleep... even deeper.

"No matter how deep you go to sleep, you are never out of touch with my voice... if you ever feel uncomfortable with your position... readjust... knowing that as you do, it helps you to relax even more.

"Now: Picture yourself in the place of your dreams... it might be a beautiful sunset on a tropical beach, perhaps a serene place in the mountains... allow yourself to go there. Imagine yourself there with your spirit guide... gently walking in the warm breeze... feel yourself getting closer to your guide... you can feel the warmth of the spirit caressing your arms, your face... you breathe in the spirit... it fills yours lungs with energy like you have never felt before. On your exhale you find yourself transformed into a higher dimension... you feel yourself flying on the wings of your spirit guide, gliding through the universe. Breathe in slowly... exhale slowly.

"Now: Picture the face of your spirit guide... the glistening eyes, the gentle smile, the whisper of the wings, the color of the aura that surrounds him/her.

"Let them guide you… help you to transform to a new level of awareness.

"Let your spirit guide bring you the answers to your questions, to guide you through your experience. Linger there for a while and allow yourself to feel free.

"Allow yourself to remain in this state for at least twenty minutes to gain the most out of your mediation."

If this script appeals to you, tape your own voice leading you through the stages to a deep meditation. There are many books written on meditation; the key is to find what works for you.

**Though these are both very good forms of meditation, I found Bill Harris's Holosync method worked best for me. You can find Bill Harris and his program at www.centerpointe.com.**

**I am giving you options here so that you can explore what is best for you and stick to it as a daily habit.**

So make a commitment right now to create your picture of achieving your dream. All great masters have taught that we become what we constantly think about. Think about your dream to the exclusion of all else, and watch your personal and professional results skyrocket!

**Take the time to understand this process. It is one of the keys to your success. Practice it until you get it. It is like magic when it starts to work. The Law of Attraction will begin to work in your favor.**

*"As you perceive something, you give birth to a thought, and this thought now thinks. Now that it exists, now that it has been conjured, now that it has been focused, now it vibrates. Now, by Law of Attraction, other thoughts that are vibrationally the same will come to it. So it begins its expansion immediately."*

**- Abraham, excerpted from the workshop in Philadelphia, PA, on Thursday, October 15th, 1998**

# WRITE YOUR VISION OR DRAW A PICTURE OF WHAT YOU WANT

# PERSONAL LIFE PICTURE

Now that you have the picture of your entrepreneurial venture, concentrate on what your life will be like once you have discovered success in your business. Do exactly what you did above and write down what you want your personal life to be. Consider areas such as relationships, health, wealth, spirituality, family, and community. Add to this picture as we go through the book. Once you start to understand how organized you can have your business or investment, you will be able to truly imagine what kind of a life you want to discover and live.

Start by doodling pictures of yourself. I use stick people for my doodles but I always have a huge smile on every one of them. It doesn't have to be perfect; it simply has to capture what you truly want.

# CHAPTER

---

## GETTING STARTED

## THE ENTREPRENEUR PROCESS

Okay, have you got your pictures and feelings in mind? Keep the picture in front of you as you move through this book. Add to them as you start to truly understand the power of imagining.

Now let's take a step together into nine S's that need to be addressed. As we travel through these areas, consider what your business venture looks and feels like today and what it will take to create the business venture you want. Compare your perfect life and the balance you are seeking with where you are now. Even if you haven't yet taken the step to try your entrepreneurial venture, you can still imagine what you really want and apply it throughout this book.

The nine S's are:

1. Strategy

2. Structure

3. Skills

4. Sense

5. Systems

6. Social

7. Spirit

8. Success

9. Sharing

In most cases, entrepreneurs understand and implement the first four S's, which are:

1. Strategy

2. Structure

3. Skills

4. Sense (measurement)

We all know businesses that spend large amounts of time describing and agreeing on a big **Strategy** and laying out how the business will be **Structured** through people and holdings. Throughout this process, they recognize the **Skills** they need and they measure their results, which I have described as **Sense**, usually in dollar amounts first, and then in some key measurement for that specific business.

Companies and businesses that don't pay much attention to the four S's I have described perish quickly because of it. I am going to take you through these four S's and give you ideas on how to ensure you are doing what it takes to get the results you imagined above.

Here are an additional five S's that will give you even better results. They are:

1. Systems

2. Social (values)

3. Spirit

4. Success

5. Sharing

These are the areas that get neglected the most, in my experience, and they can make or break an entrepreneur's business interests and the results he/she desires.

A large number of people and businesses fail to consider the **Systems** they have or don't have in place. The **Social** S stands for the values, behaviors, and beliefs of the company and the people within it. **Spirit** is the essence of a business and the owner/investors; **Success** is the result of all the S's; and **Sharing** is how you actually give back in order to keep receiving.

So come along with me as we delve into the meaning of these nine S's and assist you in reaching a business experience you never dreamed of.

# CHAPTER

---

## FIRST S - STRATEGY

## WHAT IS A STRATEGY?

Strategy is your image, the big desire that you truly want for your business or investment. In order to achieve results, you need to have your strategy written down. Once it is in writing it becomes alive, and it is something that begins to take shape on paper and then in your mind. Once you have put down your desire on paper it is attracted toward you. Write the date you expect your business to be in place and successful.

Now, there can be a lot of confusion about strategy. You hear people talking about Mission, Vision, Goals, and Purpose. It is never ending and confusing. Every company has a different definition of each word, and many have a different take on what they are intended to do.

This book uses Strategy to get you started in outlining your true desires. You can find some examples of Purpose, Mission, Vision, and Goals at www.successtoolbox.com so you can decide how they influence you and your ideas. You can also download a paper written by Bob Proctor called "Purpose, Vision & Goals."

# WRITING YOUR ENTREPRENEUR STRATEGY

Writing a strategy is difficult for most people. They haven't thought about their true wants, and the strategy never materializes.

YOU HAVE TO PAINT A COMPELLING FUTURE FOR OTHERS TO UNDERSTAND AND HELP YOU REALIZE YOUR DREAM.

Bob Proctor's chart has helped me to realize why that is.

| FANTASY | WHAT YOU WANT |
|---------|---------------|
| Plan | What you think you can do |
| Know | What you can achieve |

Most people spend their wholes lives in the bottom left-hand corner, knowing what they can achieve. Knowing how to do something, they remain content with the results they are getting. There is so much more that they could be enjoying.

Then, once in a while, a person will start to think they can do better, so they make a plan to improve. So in Bob's example they move to the next level. They believe they can do better. Unfortunately instead of trusting themselves and their plan they listen to their broke, unhappy friends, colleagues and family who tell them it is impossible to improve and that you will not make it. So what happens? You go right back to your old way of doing things and keeping the same old results.

This book is intended to help you write the plan and then take the tools being offered in the book to ensure you take your plan to the next level, a fantasy of what you truly want, and stay there.

In order to stretch and reach past your present results, you must have a **Fantasy.**

## WHAT DO YOU WANT?

Go back to the picture you painted above for your business venture and your strategy and personal life. You have described it, and now this book will assist you in learning key tools and finding the courage to get it.

You need to stretch to have a big fantasy, just as I asked you to create a picture of what you want. You must realize what you really want and what you have to do to break through your fear to reach that level. That is why building a clear big strategy will guide you to the pinnacle of success.

Writing this book was a big stretch for me, and I was often afraid, thinking I wasn't good enough to write a book – who would buy it, and who was I to think I had the ideas to help others succeed? Well, writing down what I wanted and the people I wanted to attract into my life made me realize that I do have what it takes to succeed, and this book being published proves it.

## WORKING THE LAWS

There are precise laws of this universe, and the one I want to become your best friend is the **Law of Attraction**. There are other laws which have been well laid out by Raymond Holliwell in his book *Working With The Law*. I highly recommend his book, which helps you to discover eleven laws that govern our results. Understanding these will enhance your life and give you success in everything you attempt.

The Law of Attraction is one that is critical to understand. It has helped me to become more and more successful as I study and apply this Law to my daily business and personal life.

The movie *The Secret* is a phenomenon that was released this past year. It has brought people together from all over the world to share how the Law of Attraction has created wealth, health, better relationships, spirituality, and balance for each of the people on the CD. For more information, visit my website at www.successtoolbox.com and connect to this powerful guide to understand this Law.

ASK YOURSELF THE FOLLOWING:

1. Do you have a clear strategy?

2. Is it written down?

3. Where are you in respect to your strategy's results?

4. Where do you want to be?

5. How do you presently plan your strategy?

6. How often do you formulate a strategy?

7. How do you predict where you will be in six months, one year, three years, and five years?

8. Where do you plan your strategy?

9. Are you the only one involved in your strategy?

10. Do you have mentors and people you trust to help you develop the strategy?

11. Who else do you involve?

12. Does this strategy represent the business concept YOU truly want?

If you have an established business, look at what you visualized and ask yourself: does it even come close to what your strategy is today? If not, what can you do about it?

If you are just starting this process as an entrepreneur, go back through the list and start to invite people whom you respect to help you formulate a clear vibrant strategy. Here are some ideas to consider.

# DEVELOPING A STRATEGY PROCESS

You must build a big strategy. Once you have a BIG STRATEGY in place, the next phase is to build smaller strategies and plans that will allow everyone working with you to understand what part they will play in the accomplishment of your business. This also helps you to be clear if you are doing it alone. You must know and help people understand their piece of the puzzle in the business venture.

Over the years, I have had the privilege of working with some very bright people on different ways to approach a strategy that can involve everyone in a business venture. One person was Dr. Barry Bebb. He was a consultant we hired at the Alberta Research Council and was a past vice president of the Xerox Corporation. He really understood a system called Hoshin Kanri, which is a systems approach to the management of change in critical business processes using a step-by-step planning, implementation, and review process. Hoshin Kanri improves the performance of business systems.

He helped us to develop the following process.

## STRATEGIC DIRECTION

*The image that you decide on*

## SUCCESS CRITERIA

*Goals that you set for the year*

## SHORT-TERM PLAN

*What you will accomplish and by when and
how you will accomplish it*

## PERFORM PLANNED WORK

*Action steps to get it done*

## AUDIT/MONITOR

*Measurement and checking whether you are on track*

**CORRECTIVE ACTION**

*Adjusting as needed*

The wheels on the bottom of this process represent the business venture aligned with the strategy. Every person has clear success criteria, short-term plans and they know how to go about contributing to the success of the company. They are empowered to make the changes needed to make it better. Throughout this, there is a communication system that keeps everyone in the loop.

# IDEAS TO CONSIDER

Planning a strategy needs to be influenced by out-of-the-box thinking. Consider going to a location that inspires you. My best work has been in Hawaii and the Rocky Mountains. There is nothing as incredible as being surrounded by God's beauty and creating within that beauty.

Do you have people whom you can turn to for help? One of the key successes for my business has been my involvement in Mastermind Groups.

What is a Mastermind Group? Napoleon Hill's book, *Think and Grow Rich*, clearly defines this process. His definition of a Mastermind is "the co-ordination of knowledge and effort, in a spirit of harmony between two or more people for the attainment of a definite purpose." He also states, "No two minds ever come together without, thereby, creating a third, invisible, intangible force which may be likened to a third mind."

I have met with people from all around the world over the phone – some from Austria, the United Kingdom, the United States, and Canada. For the past three years, I have participated in a Mastermind Group with people from Michigan, Florida, and Texas. We have studied Napoleon Hill's *Think and Grow Rich* twice now and have learned to apply his principles in everything we undertake, both business and personal.

As a result, each of us has a clear strategy to follow. We have each defined our life's purpose, and each of us has a written plan to follow and to share weekly with one another. We share our wins for the week and ask for support from the group for the following week. When several people with like-minded thoughts come together to share out loud, the results are unbelievable. We have watched ourselves grow and prosper because of the support of the group.

One key aspect of our Mastermind is the fact that each of us has defined out true purpose in life. On the SuccessToolbox web site I have included an article written by Lisa Rigato about Purpose. Lisa is a Purpose Coach and truly understands how to help people realize their true purpose in life. Go to www.daystarvisionsinc.com to experience what this wonderful woman has to offer.

My dear friend Colin Markin leads many Masterminds and encourages others to build their own groups for study and support as they succeed in their business and personal lives.

To know more about Masterminds and to find one you can join, visit www.successtoolbox.com.

# BECOMING WHO YOU ASSOCIATE WITH

Have you surrounded yourself with winners? Who are your friends? Are they successful in business, in health, and in happiness? If not, you are spending time with people who will drag you down with their thoughts, as good-intentioned as they are. My publisher and friend, Gerry Robert, advised me to surround myself with people I wish to emulate, here and elsewhere. Offer your help to people who you want to emulate. Copy them. If they are getting great results, you will learn from being around them the habits that are taking them to the top.

Invite people whom you admire to meet with you to develop your strategy. Take them to a different location and help them visualize your business together.

Height can be an out-of-the-box influence for people. At my previous position for the Alberta Research Council, we took our senior team to the top of the gondola at Lake Louise, Alberta. Imagine looking out over the mountaintops to consider a bigger and better Alberta Research Council.

As we sat at the top of the world planning our strategy, a huge storm formed on the horizon and quickly engulfed the tower we were in. It poured rain, and then as suddenly as it began, it stopped, and a vivid rainbow stretched across our vista. There wasn't a person in that room who couldn't start to imagine in vivid color what we wanted for our business strategy.

We have also taken our team to the past at Fort Edmonton Park. This allowed us to reminisce about the past before we planned for the future. It gets obstacles out of the way early and sets a new course to the future.

If you are building a franchise with people working for you, then there will be a defined process that you will be required to follow. The reason for this is that it works. It has a proven track record, and by following it, you will be successful. But just because it is proven doesn't mean that it can't be improved. Involve your people in looking for better and new ways to do business. You also need to ensure that the strategy is on target and that people are thoroughly oriented to it and following it.

## DOING THE OPPOSITE OF OTHERS

One lesson our Mastermind is quickly learning from reading and studying the book *The Four Hour Work Week*, by Timothy Ferriss, is to do the opposite of what others are doing. So whatever type of business or investment you decide on, consider doing it opposite of the way others are doing it.

Let me share with you a personal example. When Curt and I got together, I had a Registered Retirement Savings Plan (RRSP)of $50,000. It had never grown in the ten years that I had it; sometimes it went down and then it would go up, but it never became more than what it was worth, despite the fact that one of the leading investment companies was helping me with it. Well, we had a dream – a little bit of heaven on a lake twenty-five minutes from Sherwood Park. It was a cottage on the lake! We cashed in the RRSP and purchased our dream cottage. Now, the investment company was very upset with me for cashing it in, but I decided to do the opposite of what others were doing, and now I am enjoying life. By the way, we had an offer of $500,000 for our cottage and land on the lake this year.

## COMMUNICATION IS CRITICAL

One of the most effective ways I have found to communicate is through pictures. Participants in my classes are asked to draw pictures of their jobs on paper plates. I tell them to put their job title in the middle of the plate and then to write down, in a creative way, all the responsibilities, tasks, and projects that they perform each day. Then I ask them to identify their top three highest priorities. People are amazed when they are done because people with similar jobs seem to have different priorities and in some cases are doing different tasks.

When you try this you may get it bang on if you have guided people through the S's I have shared with you in this book. If not, this is the perfect place to start talking about what should be on their plate. It will also help people who think you do nothing all day truly understand what you are doing and why.

You can have the best strategy in the world, but if no one knows about it, you have nothing. I have been in hundreds of companies, and this is the critical factor that keeps them from total alignment and success: COMMUNICATION!

When you are planning your business venture or investment, consider how much the people on the front line know. We all believe we know how to communicate and that others understand what we say and want. We know that everyone is listening to what we have to say. Really?

If there is anything that will give you success, it is timely, informative, clear, and inspiring communication between you and anyone involved in your business venture. This includes you, customers, employees, partners, co-workers, investors, and anyone I have left out.

Active listening comprises 70 percent of good communication. Taking the time to really listen to others will move you forward more quickly than you can imagine. A company with which I am consulting this year has a president who insists that everyone get to know their people. This is so important. Getting to know who you are working with, what turns them on, and what inspires them will help you to plan your dream with the best of intentions and results. You will be linked in and able to lead anyone to the finish line.

# WHAT GETS IN THE WAY OF COMMUNICATING?

The more layers you add to a business venture, the more you block communication. I will talk about this in the next chapter on structure, but I want to stress that people tend to want to hold onto their power, and whether they mean to or not, they tend to use knowledge as their leverage. Please be aware of this and take the obstacles to communication out of the way.

In any business venture or team there are leaders and a vision-keeper. By this, I mean that there are always one or two people who hold the vision for you, sometimes even if you do not quite understand it. If they forget to share and communicate effectively to new people, the business will be unable to flourish because new people will not know where the business is going or how they fit into the plan. How are you going to effectively communicate the plan and how will each person in the organization fit into that plan?

Involving respected people within the business to help communicate the plan is one way to ensure that everyone knows what is expected and where they are going. Pick people from different parts of the team to assist in communicating and planning the implementation stage of the strategy. Find the leaders and then assist them in helping others to understand.

One way we changed our habit of communication at the Alberta Research Council was by requiring senior management to meet with a department once a month on a Friday. There was no way to get out of it. At first the departments were really nervous and had huge amounts of research and data to share with us. Then they realized that we were there to ask them how it was going, what questions they had about our strategy and goals for the year, what obstacles were getting in their way, and how were they doing. Once everyone understood this, the communication opened and people were on the same page, understanding how they fit into the company direction.

If you are building a network marketing business, communication is a key ingredient in the success of your team. How will you communicate to others, usually around the globe, without wearing yourself out? Also, as you try to communicate over and over, how will you keep the message vibrant so that people want to read or hear your message? Today we are overwhelmed with useless information; people share unimportant details and stories just for the sake of talking. E-mail has become a nightmare for some companies and the people who work within them.

One of the keys to success is to build a team that is creative, not competitive, and to ensure that there is a communication method to which people will pay attention and with which they will want to be involved.

I have found that developing a weekly communication process works. It can be a telephone conference call or a conference room on the Internet where you can share PowerPoint slides as well as talk. People on your team will become a vital part of this meeting and be willing to come forward with ideas that are working and ones that aren't working, so you can help the entire team adjust to a better way of doing business. Let different people run the call and bring new ideas to the table.

If you are building your own business venture, WHERE YOU ARE IT, communication with yourself is critical. You must think about what you are thinking and how you are going to attract business to yourself. Now, what do I mean by "think about what you're thinking?" Just that! Start to listen to what you say to yourself. I ask my coaching clients to write daily in a journal everything they are saying to themselves over a week. You would be surprised what you hear. One successful gentleman whom I was coaching called me to say that he was saying some terrible things to himself. Once you are aware of what you are thinking, you can change it and enhance positive thoughts.

## PERSONAL STRATEGY

Now, what about your personal strategy? How does that fit with what you are planning in your business ventures? This is where you start to work smarter, not harder, and find a balance that will allow you to enjoy your life, your family, your friends, and time alone to renew yourself.

```
    #30  11-20-2010 12:25PM
tem(s) checked out to TURCONI, SEAN R.

ITLE: The success toolbox for entrepren
ARCODE: 38138001628241
UE DATE: 12-11-10

ITLE: Marketing without advertising
ARCODE: 38138001717788
UE DATE: 12-11-10

ITLE: Ultimate guide to search engine o
ARCODE: 38138001611593
UE DATE: 12-11-10

ITLE: Keeping the books : basic recordk
ARCODE: 38138001359599
UE DATE: 12-11-10

TITLE: Broke : the plan to restore our t
BARCODE: 38138001812928
DUE DATE: 12-04-10


        CHICOPEE PUBLIC LIBRARY
            413-594-1800
```

# WHAT SHOULD YOU BE CONSIDERING?

Alberta, at present, is in an economic boom. Everyone has his/her head down, concentrating on making money. I hear people say all the time, "I don't take vacations; there isn't time." Really? When will there be time – when you are old and unable to travel? When you have burnt yourself out and couldn't enjoy anyone's company if you tried? I see it all around me – people unable to eat a meal without talking on their cell phones, never having a moment to feed their bodies and souls. People sit on the beach on vacation with the cell phone ringing every five minutes. The plane touches down, and they announce that you can now use your cell phone. Why? You call that balance? We are a society that has reached a critical moment of never having time to ourselves. You must plan it, and you must take it.

What do you want in your life? Do you want to be in control of what, when, and where you go and do? If you are going to succeed in business, you must succeed in your personal life. You have to refresh yourself and stay focused on the things that matter the most to you.

As I described previously, Curt and I have a piece of paradise on Islet Lake just twenty-five minutes from where we live in Sherwood Park, Alberta. We have a pact. The weekend starts on Friday afternoon and ends on Monday morning at the cottage, surrounded by God's beauty. Soon we will be living there during the summer to enjoy Alberta's sunshine, nature, and peace.

Make some decisions early on to decide how you want to live your life. Yes, you have to take action in your business, but planning the outcome of both your business and personal life is a sure-fire way to make it become a reality.

# CHAPTER

---

## BUILDING THE RIGHT STRUCTURE

## STRUCTURE

Structure refers to the way your business venture is set up. Are you the President, CEO, and Chief Bottle Washer? Then your structure is you, and you are going to develop the big and small strategies for your success.

This is what it will look like for you: A session I attended this year claimed that when you are alone in a business, it is important to write out all the duties you perform. We are in an entrepreneurial explosion, with thousands of businesses starting up each year, and by year four only 7 percent of those businesses are still in business. Why? Because we try to do it all ourselves, and it becomes an overwhelming task.

I am asking you to identify each business position within your business venture. Now, on a flip-chart list the positions and write the name of the person currently doing the work. If you are the only person, put your name in each position that requires your direct attention.

It will look like this:

| President | Market | CFO | Sales | Janitor | Reception | Books |
|-----------|--------|-----|-------|---------|-----------|-------|
| **Me** | **Me** | **Me** | **Me** | **Me** | **Me** | **Me** |

As your business grows, you will want to consider who you need to bring on board to assist you. **YOU CAN'T CONTINUE TO DO IT ALL YOURSELF.** You can consider hiring someone as a consultant, a mentor, a coach, or in a full-time position. Maybe you want partners to take over the running of the business venture to free you up for more fun. What is the maximum effort that you can handle? Identify this, and you will know what you need to do. Later in my book, the key ingredient of balance also becomes part of this equation.

# SPECIALIZED KNOWLEDGE

Know where to find specialized knowledge. I highly recommend that you read Napoleon Hill's *Think and Grow Rich* to understand the importance of knowing when and where to find the specialized knowledge that you need.

Henry Ford overcame poverty, illiteracy, and ignorance by aligning himself with great minds and absorbing their thoughts into his. With the assistance of a Mastermind Group, Henry Ford had at his command all the specialized knowledge he needed in order to be successful.

Napoleon Hill wrote, "Any person is educated who knows where to get knowledge when it is needed and how to organize that knowledge into definite plans of action."

Some of the companies that I have worked for are owned by families. In most cases, the following hierarchical structure is the way they have set up the company. A lot of larger companies have structured themselves this way, neglecting to explore other options because it is too hard to redirect "the ship."

EXAMPLES: Hierarchical Structure of Business

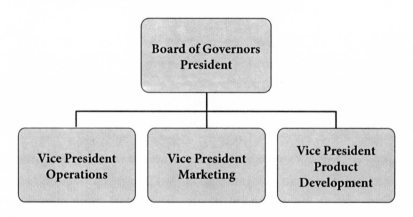

And on and on it goes until it reaches the person working in one department, far down into the depths of the company. In between are the managers and supervisors who hold onto their power and actually get caught in the game of impeding success as they hold on to what is theirs. Unless you are crystal clear about outcomes, this structure causes some major road blocks, and communication becomes a real problem within the corporation if it is not thought through clearly.

# TEAM

This approach can bring great gains to you and your business. It involves people working together in harmony and creativity, solving problems and respecting one another, and people having responsibility for business outcomes and for keeping the customer happy.

# MASTERMIND

This is a coming together of the minds. Different minds don't have to be in the same location, but they must be in harmony with your definite purpose and the strategy for what you are trying to achieve. Once this becomes effective, you will not believe the results you can attract through others.

## SEAMLESS

Having a seamless structure that involves people all over the world is a great strategy. When I consider some of the network marketing companies that have this working for them, Nikken stands out. Nikken is in dozens of countries with a corporate presence, communicating and coordinating efforts. There are true leaders who ensure people are well-educated about the strategies and processes of the head office. People are working in teams and supporting one another all over the world.

## WHAT ELSE IS MISSING?

Structure refers to much more than who reports to whom and who is in charge. You need to consider what other pieces of your structure are missing to ensure your future success.

- Do you have a legal firm that is working on your behalf?

- Do you have your business legalities in line?

- Are fiduciary responsibilities clearly outlined?

- Is your structure legally sound?

- Do you have an accounting firm that works for you?

- Can you count on them for advice and for strategic planning with respect to taxes and tax incentives?

- Do you need a Board of Directors?

- Do they have clear direction as to their responsibilities?

- Do you have a support network in place?

- Do you have a coach?

- Do you have mentors to turn to?

- Are they trusted advisors to give you guidance?

- Are there leaders to look up to and to model your organization after?

- Do you have shareholders to whom you are accountable and who bring value to their shares?

- Do you have investors?

- Who are your internal customers?

- Who are your external customers, and how are you structured to be accountable to these customers?

- Who are your suppliers?

- Are they considered in your structure and part of the way you do business?

- Are they aligned with your business and strategy?

The questions above are important indicators of how your structure should be aligned with your strategy. The structure of your organization depends on the type of business and your need for control.

Is it time to consider changing your current business structure into a new structure that will better meet the needs of your strategy and get better results?

# COMMUNICATION AGAIN

Again, I am going to talk about communication. Curt and I have invested in some companies and never received a single word of communication from them as they used our money for their dreams. We have been involved in a public company, private companies, start-up companies, and passive income investments. Some of these investments communicate on a monthly basis and hold an annual general meeting, and some do not. Some we have never heard from again. Boy, have we learned to ask the questions in this book before we get involved. Demand some form of communication, especially when it is your money that they are using to get the business venture started. When you are running the business, remember to communicate back to your investors in some way.

## REMEMBER THE BUSINESS VENTURE YOU IMAGINED?

Does that business fit with the way you are presently aligned? Well, what will it take to get you where you want to go?

Bob Proctor often talks about his head office in Scottsdale, Arizona, where the majority of his team serves his company worldwide, AND HE HAS ONLY VISITED THE OFFICE ONCE. What does that say about this incredible man and his company? He built a team, and he expects them to be a team without his interference. However, he clearly understands the skills he needs before he hires a team of people to work with him – which brings me to the next S: **SKILLS.**

*Build the right business for you. Make it work for you. Think out of the box when you are attracting people toward you.*

*"Every company has two organizational structures: The formal one is written on the charts; the other is the everyday relationship of the men and women in the organization."*

**– Harold S. Green**

# CHAPTER

---

## SKILLS

## RECOGNIZING AND APPLYING SKILLS

Picking the right people for the right job is the hardest task of all. If we could all be like ourselves we wouldn't have to second guess, right? Wrong – if we were all like ourselves we wouldn't get anything done because we can't do it all by ourselves. The fact is that you need a blend of motivated people with positive attitudes, great values, and competencies that match the job you are asking them to do. This applies equally to network marketing, owning a franchise, and owning a business.

Most business people are so busy keeping the business afloat that they tend to hurry over the important task of hiring the right person for the right job.

One corporation that brought me in to consult on its hiring practices had previously promoted people into jobs without providing any training or educational support. Placing people in jobs for which they lack the appropriate skills leads to many serious problems in a company.

Throughout my career, I have been privileged to mentor people to their highest level. The ability to recognize strengths and weakness in others and to be able to coach people to a higher level has always been my joy. I believe that to help others succeed through personal and business growth is an entrepreneur's duty.

Hiring people based on behaviors and values is the key to success. There are many companies that have developed a specialized method to help you find the right people for your business.

## SUGGESTING A PROCESS

When you are picking the right people for the job, start by asking them to lay out their skills and to describe which skill they particularly love to do. People will be most motivated to do what they truly love to do.

Start with the job that you are expecting that person to do. So, for example, if a person is an inside sales person, you want to imagine how that person will interact with others, what kind of image they will portray for the company, how they will impress and serve customers, and what kind of people skills they will need. Do they know how to smile and shake hands? I cannot say enough about hand-shaking. There are so many people in important jobs with whom I shake hands and know immediately that they are insecure. A handshake is a first contact with someone, and it needs to be confident and sure.

If the job is a network marketing position, take the time to lay out the process that is required to be successful. Most network marketing companies have a clear process laid out, but there is always room for improvement. Don't hesitate to turn your business into one that works for you.

Many companies use an outside Human Resources department that does the hiring for them, or the company has a clear hiring process that they apply when hiring new people. I have been in a franchise restaurant where the manager is sitting with some new person applying for the job. He/she is interviewing in the middle of the restaurant with people and noise all around and expects that he/she will be able to pick the right person for the job!

If you own a business, when was the last time your Human Resources people upgraded their skills? They need to do so in order to understand the types of people who are needed in today's marketplace and which resources are available to them. When was the last time you sat down with the Human Resources people and talked about changing needs and the type of people you want to hire to take your company to a higher level?

When was the last time you updated a list of your skills? We are always learning new things, and if you don't write them down, you may forget. If you are not continually learning, then you are standing still and in fact sliding backwards. I encourage people to keep a success journal so they can look back at what new skills they have acquired and what they have achieved in their business venture.

The Skills step is so critical to your organization. If you have a Human Resources department, make sure they understand what you want and need for your organization.

## IF YOU ARE DOING THE HIRING YOURSELF, HERE IS A PROCESS TO FOLLOW:

What position do you need to be filled? Is it permanent, part-time, or contract?

What are your expectations for these positions? Write down what you want your new employees to achieve.

One franchise company in Edmonton encourages their staff to recommend new employees. Remember, if you are hiring the best, they are probably spending time with others who are just as good.

Describe in your own words what your new employees will do in their positions to move the company forward. Tell a story about each position. Imagine what they will do, why they will do it, how they will do it, where they will do it, and for whom they will do it. Think out of the box, because this description becomes a starting point for discussion with a new applicant.

Once you know the position and the skills required, start to describe the behaviors you want the employee to have within that position. **Peel the onion** in describing your behaviors for the workplace.

For instance, many business people say they want someone that has the behaviors of a **team player**. Well, what does that look like? What does it mean to be a team player?

You might consider a team player a person who:

- Takes initiative

- Solves problems

- Is solution based

- Takes the customer's point of view

- Works collaboratively with people in other functions

- Communicates necessary information to others in a clear and timely manner

- Makes decisions

- Gets along well with others and has a positive attitude

- Listens to others

- Contributes improvements to the team

- Leads by example and demonstrates what he/she says and believes in

- Demonstrates flexibility

- Loves to learn

You must be willing to peel the onion in every position. The end result is true clarity about both the position and the person best suited for that position. There are some things that can be taught, so be willing to coach and mentor people in the areas that they have not yet mastered.

Do not ignore identifying the behaviors you want in your business. You can hire a person with incredible credentials, but he/she might turn out to be a tyrant who no one likes to work with or for.

A test that I apply is to go into a company and interview the employees. I ask them what they like about the company and what they don't like. Invariably, the list of what they don't like is easier and longer. In reality, that list is important because it shows the behaviors that everyone really wants in the company.

For example, the complaint might be that employees talk behind each other's backs, but the reality is that the employees want open communication in which people can talk about their concerns and find solutions to their problems.

Please, please be prepared to list acceptable behaviors and to fire people who disregard the behaviors asked of them. Nothing undermines a company more than having people say one thing and do another.

This brings me back to Strategy, Structure, and Skills. They all must work together. Dr. Barry Bebb, our consultant at the Alberta Research Council, always talked about bringing people in an organization Face to Face, Heart to Heart, and Mind to Mind.

**Face to Face** means that people are willing to talk to one another, even through hard subjects.

**Heart to Heart** means that people care enough about each other to show respect, to listen, and to honor others' ideas.

**Mind to Mind** is the ultimate level where people come together and are aligned in their ability to think and create harmonious solutions and ideas that will take the company's strategy over the top.

So, in summary, skills are not just education and experience based, but they include the behaviors that your organization needs to achieve its strategic goals.

Now, identifying the behaviors you need takes work and time. Decide if you have the time and if not, **hire someone** to help you do it. But be sure to be perfectly clear about what you want and need for each position. Initially, this will be work for you, but it will pay off in a huge way later.

# CULTURE OF LIFE-LONG LEARNING

At many points in an entrepreneur's business venture there will be the need to learn new skills. Developing a culture of learning becomes essential to keeping your business on the cutting edge.

I have worked as a consultant over the past 12 years with Achieve Global Canada, a world leader in helping organizations translate business strategies into business results by developing the skills and performance of their people. As a training facilitator, I have offered *Professional Training Skills* and *Leadership for Results* sessions to many organizations in Alberta, Saskatchewan, and British Columbia. Learning skills based on leadership and sales expertise has helped people to hone what they have and to gain new knowledge and skills to meet corporate expectations and business outcomes.

Be prepared to encourage life-long learning in any business investment or endeavor that you undertake. Lead by example.

Encourage and coach your workforce, your partners, and your investors to lead this strategy as a major success factor for your enterprises.

# SKILLS SUCCESS STORY

Let me introduce you to Bruce Kirkland, General Manager of Lexus of Edmonton. Bruce is an entrepreneur and has a talent for hiring the right people for his business. He understands the importance of hiring the right person for the right position.

**Janis:** How do you define yourself as an entrepreneur based on the definitions in my book?

**Bruce:** The most important thing is that you have to have a vision and you have to have a passion. As you know, when I came to the car business, I had no idea about the car business. I couldn't even tell you what the symbols on the back of the car were or what they meant. I don't think it's important that you have the knowledge of the product, but you have to have a passion to learn it, a passion for people, and a drive to succeed. It can't all be about profit, but certainly you have to have a plan, you have to see the big picture, you have to take responsibility, and you have to take stewardship of it. I think that's really critical. When I came here, my real desire for Lexus was my passion to make sure it was going to be successful. Those skills are transferable from the car business to retail business or any business, if you have the passion and if you have some ideas or plans about how to manage and operate a business. Don't be afraid; be an entrepreneur. If you don't know anything about running a candy store, you can still learn it.

**Janis:**   Thank you, Bruce; that's why I included the description of people already working in industries who don't realize that they are entrepreneurs and who are just not willing to have the courage to step out and do it for themselves or attract others to help them do it.

**Bruce:** As you know, when I got offered this job, I turned it down three times because, as I said to the ownership group here, I didn't know anything about cars. One of my business mentors leaned over to me and said, "Bruce, it's not really about cars, is it? It's about people."

**Janis:** So what role has this played in building Lexus of Edmonton into the top dealership in Canada? How do you think you've done that, Bruce?

**Bruce:** I'm going to say a couple of things. I think my passion to succeed – because I do have a passion to succeed – has been important. And no matter what business I've been in, I've succeeded in it because of my passion and the drive inside. But I think the key here is really my greatest asset – my people. Entrepreneurs should always surround themselves with good people. And if you do surround yourself with good people, you are going to be successful. I have a very strong business philosophy that I like to surround myself with people who are stronger than me, and I'm not afraid to do that. If you do that, you are going to be successful.

At Lexus I have surrounded myself with great people, and I let them do their jobs. I knock the roadblocks down for them, but I also recognize and reward them continually. I think that's one thing entrepreneurs sometimes don't do. Because we're entrepreneurs, we recognize ourselves, but we don't recognize the people around us. I think you should recognize and reward your people continually.

I also believe that you need structure and some standard operating procedures (SOPs) in place. You can't just fly by the seat of your pants when you are an entrepreneur because you are going to get in trouble that way. You also need the right people. I want people to want my job. I want someone to be sitting in my manager's chair. So if I have three or four young people that want it, I know that they are going to be working very hard, and if I am rewarding and recognizing them all the time, they are going to stay with me and succeed. So I think our success at Lexus of Edmonton and my success as a manager result from having the best people, no question. And I've got people who have no car experience, Janis, as you know. I went out purposely and got people who had no car experience.

**Janis:** Bruce, just talk a little bit about how you went about selecting the people with the right skills who work with you.

**Bruce:** It was an interesting process because when I got the job and decided I would be general manager, we ran an ad in the *Edmonton Journal* that said we needed the following positions. I started interviewing and I was appalled. I thought, I'm not hiring any of these people I'm interviewing. I knew the type of people and skills that I truly wanted, and so I decided to use my networking groups – I belong to a lot of networking groups. I said, "We're looking for good people. Do you know any?" When we started the process I was looking for people who had a great attitude: people who really put people in front of the product, people who told me they had a passion to serve others. If they talked about how they knew more about cars or knew more about metal, I didn't hire them. I hired people from outside the industry, but I looked for people who wanted to be part of a team. I challenged them to be part of a team. I wanted to know what kind of passion they had for life – not only for work, Janis – but what their passions were outside of work. So I was blessed, and I got a lot of really, really great people. And my service writers who couldn't tell you what a brake pad was are both ladies. One came from the hair dressing industry and one ran her own store. People thought I was crazy to hire these two people who knew nothing about cars, but guess what? They have a passion to serve people. You can always learn about brake pads.

**Janis:** Of course you can!

**Bruce:** But if you have the skill to care about people, it is a natural skill that you possess. You can always acquire the computer skills. I looked for people to be part of a team, people who wanted to serve, and people who really had a passion. So I was blessed.

**Janis:** So when you talk about a team, how do you define the behaviors that you're looking for with those people working in that team, Bruce?

**Bruce:** The most important behavior is that we support each other, that we are part of a team, and that no one is more important than the team. I'm not a big believer in the idea that "I'm the general manager and I'm not going to do what others do;" when you are an entrepreneur and starting a business, make sure that you do everything. I think it's important at the start of a team that everyone has to learn every part of the business. If I expect you to work late, I'm going to work late. As a mentor, you've got to show the team that you are willing to do what you are asking them to do. But I think being a team means knowing that everyone is going to support each other, but also knowing that they are going to get support from me and the executive team because in the end we are accountable for the results the team achieves.

If the employees get support from management, they are going to support you. Don't let them out there by themselves. If they find themselves in a tricky situation, if they make a mistake, this is the way to handle it in my view: thank them. Say, "Thank you for trying so hard, that was great," talk about what was learned from the experience and then correct the mistake. But always remember that they are trying to help you!

**Janis:** So what I hear you saying is that you lead by example. You don't care about getting your hands dirty. If your employees have to do it, you're going to do it.

**Bruce:**  Absolutely. Respect is earned, not given. Sometimes I think that when people start a business, they think, "Well, I'm the owner here." Big deal; you're the owner. It's not important that you're the owner; the important thing is that your team and the people around you see you first as a part of the team and see that you are going to support them and that you're going to work. I don't lead my store by saying, "I'm the owner, do as I say." I certainly don't lead that way. I lead my store while standing beside my employees – not in front of them, and not behind them pushing, but right beside them.

**Janis:**  How do you build a compelling future for your team?

**Bruce:**  We circulate an internal monthly newsletter in which I talk about our goals and what we're doing. Every first Saturday of the month, we have a kick-off meeting for our sales team, which I personally lead. I give members the big picture on where we're going, how the "ship" is doing, what we're doing right, and what we're working on. I get their input.

We have a committee here called the Lexus Experience Committee and we meet monthly. They come up with ideas as to how we can improve the store; they tell me, you know, we're falling down here. I give them some ownership. I let them know that they are part of the process of goal-setting. I listen to them. If you can treat them like a family and if you're honest with them, they are going to help.

They'll buy in. They want to be successful. We are the number one store in Canada, and every year I say, "Do we want to do this again next year?" They say, "Absolutely!" Well, how are we going to get there? I could tell them how to get there, Janis, but it's more important that they tell me how we're going to get there, because they know. If I'm listening, they are going to own it more than if I say, "These are the five things we need to work on..."

**Janis:** This is the key – that you listen and implement their ideas, which I think a lot of people forget to do. They listen to their employees, but then they tend to ignore their suggestions.

**Bruce:** Exactly. Or the team calls you into a special meeting for two hours, or you spend half a day planning, putting this document together, and it goes into a binder and is placed on a shelf. Then next year, you pull it out, blow the dust off of it, and ask your staff to come back and give you input again. Well, they look at you and say, "We gave you input last year that you didn't even look at, so why are we doing it again?"

In the newsletter, we have a goal for the month or a saying for the month or a value for the month, so we all know what we are trying to do this month. For instance, Jordan came up with this great idea, and we're going to try it this month and see how it goes.

Also, whenever I receive an email from one of our Lexus guests who compliment one of the staff, no matter what it was, I give them a gift. For instance, last week Raylene did a great job with this guest in service. I received the email and pulled out a pair of Oiler hockey tickets and said to Raylene, "I'm just so impressed. Mr. Jones just emailed me about what a great job you did for him." Or I might give the employee a gift certificate to take his/her family out to dinner. We do something like that every time someone from the outside recognizes one of our staff. We also have an employee-of-the-month program here to try to build the team.

**Janis:**  Recognition is built right into your culture.

**Bruce:** It has to be built into the culture. That is why when people come in here, they can feel the power of people who have been recognized, they know our team takes ownership of their responsibilities and cares about how they treat the customer. That's really the key. People tell me all the time, "It's a different feel here at Lexus." And it IS a different feel.

**Janis:**  I know what you mean, as Curt and I have experienced it many times. Bruce, when you say "the feel," what does that mean to your customer walking in? What is the difference? What feeling do they get walking into your dealership?

**Bruce:** I think they get a feeling that they are walking into a home rather than a car dealership. People are going to sit down and say hello and get to know them and really care about them and not worry about the car. They are going to talk to them about their lives and where they're going. The guests are always greeted very quickly. It's very comfortable; there are places to sit, there's a fireplace, and there are all sorts of things that help the feel. But it's the way people talk to you; they are genuine. It's the sense that they really care. Janis, I think you know when people care or don't care – you know whether it's phony or not phony – and I think our people really believe that they should welcome you. It doesn't have to be your salesperson.

Anyone will sit down and talk to you here, and I think that's the important thing. We call you guests, not customers, because you're in our house.

**Janis:** Both Curt and I have experienced that with you, Bruce. Can I ask you, then, what do you think is the one main reason for your business success?

**Bruce:** I think that as an entrepreneur, you can never give just one reason for your success; I think it's a combination of elements. I tell people I'm putting a jigsaw puzzle together here, Janis, and the pieces all have to fit. Lots of times I've interviewed people who are very, very strong but wouldn't fit into a team, and so I wouldn't hire them. So that is my biggest success: my people. A lot of companies make great cars. BMW makes great cars, Mercedes makes great cars, and Lexus makes great cars. What differentiates us from all of those people is the way you get treated here. So my success comes from the people with whom I've surrounded myself. So maybe it is one thing.

**Janis:** That's wonderful, Bruce. I also know that what my book is trying to do is to talk about the things that have to go into a business, but also to point out that life-long learning is an important part of people's success. What do you do about life-long learning?

**Bruce:** I think it's critical, and it's interesting that you mentioned it, because I invest more in training than most dealerships ever do. I believe in training, and I bring trainers in who don't have to be in the car business. There are some great trainers in the car business. Harvey Cowen is great, and we bring him in. I think it's important that my team sees me going to functions or networking, but that they also see me going to life-long learning events. We hold training sessions for our team's personal growth plan.

Every year, I sit down with each of my staff and we talk about what they are doing personally and professionally to grow and what they are doing to improve themselves. They know that that is one question they are going to hear from me. If I don't personally do it, how can I expect them to do it? So I think life long learning is important. I will send them to a course that may not have anything to do with cars. I may send them to a course on financial planning, sales, or travel, because if employees see us investing in them, they will go the extra mile for us.

**Janis:** So you're encouraging them to be at the top of their game, no matter what it is.

**Bruce:** Yes, absolutely.

**Janis:** That's part of your reward system as well, isn't it?

**Bruce:** Absolutely.

**Janis:** If I asked you to name just a few of the books that influenced you, what would those be, Bruce?

**Bruce:** *Good to Great* by Jim Collins was a very good book. A book that I read that I really, really liked was *Winners Never Cheat* by Jon M. Huntsman. It's on my desk all the time. It's about everyday values that we learned as children but may have forgotten.

I just finished reading a book called *Filling the Glass: The Skeptic's Guide to Positive Thinking in Business*, a very good book by Barry Maher.

I think the biggest influence on the way I think and my leadership style has been my large family of eleven and the lessons that my parents taught me. They had a tremendous influence on us, teaching us that we had to be a team.

**Janis:** Bruce, is it just part of seeing business from a different perspective?

**Bruce:** That's what it is, for sure. I think that entrepreneurs need to collaborate more and network more. It's really helped me be very successful. I collaborate a lot with my team, but I am also at many, many networking events just listening to people. I call it planting a garden. You know you've got to put the seed out there and plant it, and when you plant a garden, you have to water it, and if you don't water it and weed it, it's not going to grow. I think it's important that you lead by example, and too many entrepreneurs don't lead by example. I try to model what I expect from others and care for my staff.

**Janis:** I know that, Bruce, and it shines through when I come into your business. Is there anything else you'd like to add?

**Bruce:** Always surround yourself with strong people. Don't be afraid. Entrepreneurs should not be afraid. The people I have around me are smarter than I am, and I know that and give them credit, not only privately, but in front of people as well.

I'll say, "Oh, Bob's the brains," or, "Have you met Tom? He's an outstanding salesman," or, "Have you met Sandy? She's an amazing person."

Always, always care for them, model what you believe in, and support them.

**Janis:**   Thank you so much, Bruce; that was incredible.

Curt and I each own a Lexus, and we have experienced from the people at Lexus of Edmonton what it means to be a guest and to benefit from the exceptional skills of Bruce's people.

# CHAPTER

---

## SYSTEMS

## IDENTIFYING SYSTEMS THAT WORK

Many business ventures fail to understand the significance of systems. Systems are what run your business venture and keep it going forward and meeting your customers' needs.

**You should consider in advance the systems you need for the fulfillment of your strategy.**

Think of the areas that need to be addressed:

- Communication systems, including phone, internet, conferencing, cell phones, BlackBerries, meetings

- Financial systems, including invoicing, accounts payable, reporting, break-even point

- Services/Product systems

- Marketing and Advertising systems

- Sales systems

- Production systems

- Implementation systems

- Hiring and Orientation systems

If you have been running your business, you may want to take stock of what you have in place and review areas that will help you to become more efficient.

If you are starting out, think through what you will need. Bring in experts who can lay out a plan with costs. My friend Charles Beaumont is a technology wizard and always says, "Learn to love your technology."

Some systems are worth putting money toward, especially if your service is contingent on meeting your customers' needs.

List all the systems that you have in place and then pick one or two key systems that, with improvement, would have a significant effect on your sales. This improvement process is referred to as Process Improvement and includes Standard Operating Procedures (SOP).

This step of process improvement can be expensive and time-consuming. I was fortunate to facilitate for Acklands Grainger Canada in a Canada-wide, Standard Operating Procedures (SOP) Team, which mapped and considered every process the company had in order to streamline and standardize them for the organization. The team spent countless hours designing, refining, and receiving employees' input into the final decisions. The end results included processes that were clearly described and written out for employees who were then able to align their jobs to the standard operating procedures consistently across Canada. Acklands Grainger then created positions for key people to ensure that the SOPs were kept alive and actually accomplishing what was intended in a continuous improvement process.

Let's start to consider how you build systems that become part of your business processes.

## EXAMPLES OF SYSTEMS

Here are some common examples of systems:

COMMUNICATION SYSTEM: PHONE

- How do your customers reach you?

- Is the phone system automated and designed
  to drive your customers mad?

- Is there a person on the other end for customers to talk to?

- Do your employees put all calls on voicemail?

- How quickly do employees get back to customers?

- If you have voicemail, do your employees change the message every day, every morning, every afternoon, or after hours?

- Is there an emergency number for customers to call?

- Do you use the phone for order-taking?


FIRST CONTACT SYSTEM:

- Is there a receptionist at your front door greeting people and connecting them to the right person in the business? This is the person who needs to make the most amount of money in the company because he/she is the first contact with your buyer. What do most businesses do? They hire a person and pay him/her the lowest amount of money.

- Are you the first contact person? Have you listened to yourself to hear how you are doing? Are you positive and friendly? Or do you sound hassled and uptight because of the kind of day you're having? A calm, confident voice over the phone instills trust in your customer.

WestJet, a very successful airline carrier in western Canada, knows how to answer the phone in person. At all hours of the day or night, you can reach someone on the phone with a great attitude. These people are also owners of the company, so there is something in it for each of them, as they treat their customers with total respect and a sense of fun.

It drives me mad when businesses take you through the computer-generated system: press this number and now listen to the 16 selections. I want to talk to a real person, and so will your customers.

Remember how I told you to do the opposite of others? Businesses today are more and more frequently using totally automated systems. People – customers – are getting more and more frustrated. Consider another way.

See my point? Establishing systems can take a lot of time; however, putting in effort up front is critical to customer and employee satisfaction.

My good friend Ray Guidinger from Acklands Grainger Canada always says, "Employee satisfaction equals corporate success."

## SYSTEMS DEAD OR ALIVE

If your systems are in line, your strategies cannot fail. If your systems do not support what you say you can do, you are dead.

One key area that is counterproductive to business is having meetings. Having meetings for the sake of meetings is such a waste of time. I know businesses that hold an Occupational Health and Safety meeting every week, and no one knows what the outcome is supposed to be. If you are holding meetings, make them meaningful and SHORT. Have people come to them prepared and ready to talk about what is important for the business venture and to talk about the expected outcomes for the business.

Other systems to think about include:

TECHNICAL SUPPORT:

- Who is setting up and caring for your computers?

- What controls and assistance do you have for emailing and communicating with your customers?

- Do you have a reliable support that will maintain your systems and come when you call?

DELIVERY SYSTEM:

- Where do your products come from and how do they get to your customers?

- Do you have a warehouse?

- What is your time commitment to your customers on orders?

- Are you in control of this system? If not, how do you guarantee delivery as promised?

SALES SYSTEM:

- How many sales calls do you make and receive per week?

- How do you pick which market to sell to?

- How do you keep track of your sales calls and follow-ups? Is there a system in place for tracking?

- Who are your customers? What customer target markets do you need to identify for the future? How do you accomplish this? Who are you focusing on?

- How many sales people do you need? Who sets dollar targets? Are they robust? How do you measure dollar results?

Other examples of systems include Occupational Health and Safety, Environmental Systems, Employee Growth Systems, Training and Personal Development Systems, Community Systems, and Recognition and Reward Systems.

Once you know your strategic goals, you will then know which systems, if improved, would give you the biggest bang for your buck. You want your systems to give you business outputs that move your business venture in front of the competition.

There are all kinds of companies that you can hire to help you with your Process Improvement. A word of caution: make sure you get returns on the investment. Hiring a company to help can be very expensive, so be sure that you are going to benefit from the results.

My advice to you is to ensure that everyone in the organization can describe the process of selling your services or product to your customers. Each employee should be able to describe what happens from the moment the customer approaches, walks in, calls, or emails your organization to the moment the customer receives their service or product. You especially as the entrepreneur must be clear on what steps happen because you are setting the strategy for others to follow.

This process applies both to a large business and to the one-person system.

Who takes the call? Where does it go from there? How does a customer buy from you? What departments are involved? How is the product or service delivered? Who follows up on customer satisfaction? How is the order processed through the financial department?

Everyone should understand the big buying-process picture and what part they play in it. Anyone should be able to describe the process to a customer or prospective client.

This is the "Wow Factor" for your business. Every employee needs to understand the process picture.

I like to have clients develop a process-flow map that goes on the wall for all to see. Everyone knows where they fit in the process, and occasionally someone comes up with a better idea. One computer software that helps you do this is Microsoft Visio. Involve people within and without the company to develop the process-flow map. Invite your customers to tell you how they perceive your system. That is a sure test of whether it is working or not. Remember, perception is everything. Perception includes the way I see it, the way you see it, and the way it really is.

Your employees become your biggest ambassadors if they are part of the big picture. Look at WestJet employees/owners who make it easy to talk with them at any time of the day and base their attitudes around customer satisfaction.

One of the most effective systems I have ever come across to market your business is described in Gerry Robert's *Publish Your Way to Profits* workshop. This is where my book started, and I can tell you that it works.

Gerry teaches you how to attract people to you. Consumers are changing. They are more skeptical, not as loyal, and more demanding than they used to be, and they expect you to offer them the services they want. Attract them to you using a book.

What excites me most about Gerry's system is that it provides a means of advertising that people will pay attention to; people do not throw out a book. For instance, a very professional real estate brochure is delivered to our home every month. On the front of this brochure is a picture of a real estate agent in a bowler hat. The picture has been taken by one of the top photographers in western Canada, and I throw it out every month. What a waste of money! Now, if he had sent me a booklet on the top ten ways to get more from your real estate investment, I would still have the booklet and would refer myself and others to this expert.

# CHAPTER

## SOCIAL

## FINDING THE SOCIAL SIDE

The Social S represents the values and behaviors in your business venture and your own life. Not everyone has the same values, so it is important for you to clearly state your values to your employees, customers, shareholders, and your community. You must also be prepared to understand and own your values.

I cannot stress enough the importance of understanding which behaviors you want for yourself and the people you work with. I have talked about this in the chapter on skills, but I will never stop repeating it. It is critical to the success of you and the people working with you.

## PEELING THE ONION

Here is where you must peel the onion until you are crystal clear about what you want.

Often, during my leadership classes, I ask people to tell me what behaviors they want to have in their work group. They tell me that they want loyalty, teamwork, et cetera. I ask them, "What does that mean to you?" Usually there are blank looks on their faces, and they struggle to define what they mean.

Without clearly articulated behaviors, you will have people-issues forever. We all come from different places. We have all been raised differently, and what is a value to one might not be a value to another.

By *values*, I refer to how you want people to treat each other, treat the customer, and treat the community. Values translate into behaviors that you want you and everyone working for you to demonstrate.

Are you simply in business to make money? If so, this model isn't going to work for you.

Do you expect people to give and show respect for one another? What does that look like for you? How are you going to communicate and then implement this value among your employees?

At the Alberta Research Council, we implemented a way to handle people talking about others behind their backs.

We called it the "Round Table Process." Any time someone from senior management came into my office to complain about another senior person on the team, we gathered at the round table, face to face, to talk it out with everyone present. Eventually, when anyone had something to discuss, it became second nature to do the "Round Table."

Recently, as I was facilitating *Leadership for Results* seminars with a major company in Alberta, a person talked about his favorite manager. This manager had a small round table in his office that was totally clear. When you came in to meet with him, he asked you to join him at the round table, and you had his complete attention. Wow, talk about listening to your people! It means so much to others and to yourself when you get it right the first time because you listened.

You must live your values! This is one of the hardest things to do consistently. Forgiveness is a value, and the ability to take a risk without fear of reprisal is another. If your business is going to transform itself into the dream you visualized at the beginning of this book, then employees need to be risk-takers, and you must embrace failure. It is only through failure that we learn to do better.

Have you heard the expression: "Walk the talk?" It couldn't be more applicable than here. You must lead the rest of your business. If you don't know how, ask! Take courses, hire a coach, tell people that you are not perfect but that you are working on it, and be willing to take advice from others.

Having a mentor or a coach in place for you is so important. Have him/her coach you and then give you feedback on your performance. Sincere, focused, personal development is hard to achieve, but until you become aware of what is possible, you will never reach your full potential. You will be a better person and a calmer and better leader for it, and your business will prosper because of it.

A company that I have come to know, whose products I continue to buy, is Nikken, the number one wellness company in the world. Their strategy is to have 1,000,000 registered wellness homes and 10,000 healthy millionaires by 2010. They have built their strategy on five pillars: healthy minds, healthy bodies, healthy families, healthy community, and wealth.

Their values are shared with every person who comes aboard, and the interesting thing is that they attract people with similar values, such as encouraging creation not competition, celebrating success, continuous learning together, having great respect for one another, and wealth-building around the world.

Take the time to develop the values that you want in your business venture, and go after people who have similar attributes.

Achieve Global Canada, www.achieveglobal.ca, truly understands and assists companies in identifying behaviors that you want to reinforce. I have worked with this company as a consultant for more than twelve years, helping to facilitate courses such as *Professional Selling Skills* and *Leadership for*

*Results* to large organizations. In their *Leadership for Results* program, one of the sessions, entitled "Giving Recognition," helps to identify which behaviors you should reinforce. Here is the starting point to understanding how to develop values. Write out what you need under each of these headings below.

**Organizational Goals and Objectives**

(First S – Strategy)

**What Your Group Needs to Accomplish**

(Success Criteria, Plans, Goals)

**Behaviors and Actions that Support Your Group's Work**

(Social - Values )

Achieve Global Canada

If you take this process and develop each section with the people that need to follow them, you will have people working within your business or working on contracts with you who are clear and understand what piece of the puzzle belongs to them.

I want to add something here that I believe is so important to the success of a business that hires people to work within it or that builds a team of people spread across the world. We all come from different places and learn different values. Some of us have taken a close look at ourselves and have identified values that we held because they were given to us by others. Let me give you an example.

Bob Proctor has often shared this example with his consultants and it shows where we allow others to influence our thinking.

"Consider the wife who every Thanksgiving cooked a ham for her family. Each year she would cut the end of the ham off and bake the ham to perfection. Her husband asked her why she cut the end of the ham off. She replied that they had always done it this way! In looking back at why they had always done it that way, they realized that her great-grandmother didn't have a pot big enough to hold the ham so she cut off the end of the ham."

See how we can inherit values and behaviors from others? What values do you have that you haven't closely examined to decide if they were actually your own?

# THE HAIDA CANOE

In the Vancouver International Airport there stands a four-meter high sculpture. It is magnificent, and the artist who created it was Bill Reid. It is called "Spirit of Haida Gwaii, the Jade Canoe." It even graces our Canadian $20 bill, as above.

What is extraordinary about this canoe is that it is filled with animals and small creatures. At the center of the canoe is the figure of a seer looking out to the future. That figure is you, the entrepreneur, as you build your business. At the back is an animal valiantly steering the canoe in the direction the seer has set. Mixed within the canoe are animals: an eagle, a wolf, bears, and smaller creatures. At the front is a male bear who is facing backwards. He does not want to go into a new future, but the female bear is peeking around the male bear, showing her cub the new direction they are going in. These are the people who are going to be involved in your business venture in some way.

Now, in the middle of the canoe there is some turmoil. The wolf is biting the wing of the eagle, the eagle has the bear's paw in its beak, and some of the smaller creatures are fighting for space. What is truly amazing, though, is that there are six large oars in the water; they are all at the same level, and everyone is pulling at the same speed in the direction that has been set as their goal.

What I understand from this is that not everyone you deal with will have the same values or understand other people's values. However, if you can create a compelling future for people that clearly shows what they need to do and where you are heading, they will all pull in the same direction. That is why the nine S's were designed for you – so you can clearly articulate and communicate what you want.

> *"Never does a man portray his character more vividly than his proclaiming the character of another."*

> **– Sir Winston Churchill**

# CHAPTER

## SENSE

## MAKING SENSE OF MEASUREMENT

Sense means measurement. How do you make sense of how your business venture is doing? What do you need to know to tell you what results you are getting? What business outcomes do you need to see to shape the company or business venture you are in?

Now, Bob Proctor would tell you never to focus on the present results, but to focus instead on what possibilities you can imagine and to shoot for those desires. Remember how you visualized your business at the beginning of this book? You should still clearly know what you are shooting for, and the picture should be starting to become crystal clear.

One method to keep your desires in front of you is a Goal Card. To download a Goal Card for yourself, visit www.successtoolbox.com. This Goal Card has helped me to keep focused on what I want daily. I carry it with me everywhere I go and read it at least four times a day. It keeps the light shining on my desire and success.

---

**MY GOAL**

By year 20…

I'm so happy and grateful now that...

_____

_____

_____

_____

_____

_____

Your Signature

---

One of the critical words in the Goal Card statement is *gratitude*. We must have gratitude for everything that is in our lives and businesses.

So how do you go about creating a goal that you can measure? Think about what you read at the beginning of this book. What follows next are the step-by-step actions required to reach your goal. They have been created by Napoleon Hill in the first chapter of his book *Think and Grow Rich*. Napoleon focuses on money, but you can focus on whatever you want to achieve as an entrepreneur.

### *"Transmuting desire for riches into its financial equivalent"*

**First**: *Fix in your mind the exact amount of money you desire. It is not sufficient merely to say, "I want plenty of money." Be definite as to the amount.*

**Second**: *Determine exactly what you intend to give in return for the money you desire. (There is no such reality as "something for nothing.")*

**Third**: *Establish a definite date by which you intend to possess the money you desire.*

**Fourth**: *Create a definite plan for carrying out your desire and begin at once, whether you are ready or not, to put this plan into action.*

**Fifth**: *Write out a clear, concise statement of the amount of money you intend to acquire, name the time limit for its acquisition, state what you intend to give in return for the money, and describe clearly the plan through which you intend to accumulate it.*

**Sixth**: *Read your written statement aloud, twice daily, once just before retiring at night and once after rising in the morning. AS YOU READ, SEE AND FEEL AND BELIEVE YOURSELF ALREADY IN POSSESSION OF THE MONEY.*

# MEASUREMENT THAT COUNTS

Many business ventures think that measurement only applies to the financial side. They consider, "How is our gross margin?" What is the net profit this month? How many widgets did we put out? How many customers or partners did we attract into our business this month?

Measurement needs to go much further than that. If you are building your own company, a franchise, or a network marketing company, how are your employees, team, or investors doing and thinking about the company? How do customers think? Have you measured your sense of satisfaction and theirs?

Remember talking about behaviors? Well, measuring behaviors and how people are exceeding the expectations of customers is another form of measurement. It also leads to a way to recognize yourself and people working for you. Are the behaviors and actions leading to successful business outputs?

If you are building a network marketing business, how is your downline and how is your upline? Are they motivated and still moving toward the big strategy? How do you know they are? Have you measured? Is everyone still aligned with the intent of the business?

# ALIGNING SENSE

One key concept that you can learn from Dr. W. Edwards Deming is his continual improvement process of the PLAN-DO-CHECK-ACT (PDCA) cycle.

The PDCA cycle represents an approach to continual improvement of activities. In the *Plan* stage, a plan of action is developed to address a problem. Measurement points and parameters are created and the plan is reviewed and agreed upon. In the *Do* stage, the plan is implemented. In the *Check* stage, information is collected on the measurements that have been agreed upon and actual results are compared to the expected results. In the *Act* stage, the results are analyzed and the causes of the differences between the actual and expected results are identified, discussed, and agreed upon. Corrective action is then taken.

I have used this PDCA cycle countless times to ensure that the measurement parameters I am expecting are on track and followed. When everyone in the business starts to use this process, it becomes a solution-oriented company.

*"Sub-optimization is when everyone is for himself. Optimization is when everyone is working to help the company."*

**– W. Edwards Deming**

This PDCA cycle is critical to your success. You know your big strategy, and you have smaller plans in place that get you to the strategy. You need to have a check system in place. So you make your plan and enact it. You need to establish when and how you will check how you are doing. If things are going well, then you look for ways to improve them. If things are not on track, then you change what you are doing, having learned from the experience.

Failure is okay. Learning from a mistake is so important. Many people say that they allow others to take risks, but when it comes to the end results, they penalize people for mistakes. We all need to learn. Look at children – they learn through mistakes every day of their young lives. Sometimes it can be a very simple habit needing change that will give you a better return on your investment.

So what business outcomes do you want to measure? Remember the strategies you set out! How did we do in achieving the strategies? How do we know we reached them?

How many people did we hire who matched our values and behaviors? How do we know that they are working? What is the intended attitude of the people in our business? What is my spirit? Am I full of joy because I am doing what I truly love? Is work effortless?

What systems did we implement this year that helped us to achieve our goals and exceed expectations? How did they exceed expectations? Can we learn from them?

What areas are modeling our values and why? Who are the bright lights in the business who are contributing to the success of our business?

How did we do in communicating throughout the business? What worked? What needs to be improved?

Did we have fun while we were building and growing the business? Why, and what contributed to this?

# CHAPTER

---

## SPIRIT

### BUILDING YOUR SPIRIT

What is meant by *spirit*? I am talking about your mindset, character, determination, will, strength of mind, and inner self. Some people have incredible spirit. They are positive and know exactly where they are going in life. If you take a long hard look at it, do you have the spirit that you have always wanted?

How do you learn to build your spirit? Napoleon Hill describes this so well in the second chapter of *Think and Grow Rich*. Applied to your personal spirit, this process will accelerate your entrepreneurial dreams.

# SELF-CONFIDENCE FORMULA

**First**: *I know that I have the ability to achieve the object of my Definite Purpose in life; therefore, I DEMAND of myself persistent, continuous action toward its attainment, and I here and now promise to render such action.*

**Second**: *I realize that the dominating thoughts of my mind will eventually reproduce themselves in outward, physical action, and gradually transform themselves into physical reality; therefore, I will concentrate my thoughts for thirty minutes daily upon the task of thinking of the person I intend to become, thereby creating in my mind a clear mental picture of that person.*

**Third**: *I know that through the principle of autosuggestion any desire that I persistently hold in my mind will eventually seek expression through some practical means of attaining the object back of it; therefore, I will devote ten minutes daily to demanding of myself the development of SELF-CONFIDENCE.*

**Fourth**: *I have clearly written down a description of my DEFINITE CHIEF AIM in life, and I will never stop trying until I shall have developed sufficient self-confidence for its attainment.*

**Fifth**: *I fully realize that no wealth or position can long endure unless built upon truth and justice; therefore, I will engage in no transaction that does not benefit all whom it affects. I will succeed by attracting to myself the forces I wish to use and the cooperation of other people. I will induce others to serve me because of my willingness to serve others. I will eliminate hatred,* *envy, jealousy, selfishness, and cynicism by developing love for all humanity because I know that a negative attitude toward others can never bring me success. I will cause others to believe in me because I will believe in them and in myself.*

**<u>Sixth</u>**: *I will sign my name to this formula, commit it to memory, and repeat it out loud once a day, with full FAITH that it will gradually influence my THOUGHTS and ACTIONS so that I will become a self-reliant and successful person.*

Signature: _____

The fifth point above is so important that I recommend you read this out loud once a day. It is a powerful statement of values, and you will never go wrong if you follow it to the letter and encourage the people working with and for you to apply the same principles to their lives.

## SPIRIT IN YOUR BUSINESS

Spirit also refers to the atmosphere that prevails in your business ventures. What is the intended spirit of your venture?

Let me talk about what this means to me. My husband Curt and I invest in spirit. We believe that people in rural settings should not have to be exported out of their community when they become older and need to be in a facility that can care for them. Our spirit led us to invest in a company that builds and manages rural assisted-living homes in Alberta and Saskatchewan.

We also believe that Canada is a wonderful place to live and vacation in. A lot of Canadians travel every winter to other destinations to get away from the Canadian winter, and we call them snow birds. A lot of them are baby boomers like myself and are starting to age and are experiencing more medical problems. As a result, they require more health insurance coverage when they travel out of Canada. There will come a day when they will start to stay in Canada as a solution. Now, I can hear people say, "Well, where is the sun in the winter in Canada?" We have lots of sun in Alberta – it just isn't thirty degrees Celsius in the winter.

As a result of our spirit and our Canadian pride, we have invested in a condo project in Nanaimo on Vancouver Island, British Columbia. We are creating a haven overlooking the ocean for people in other parts of Canada to own in order to get away from the harsh winters and still have their Canadian health care readily available to them.

Again let me refer to WestJet as an example of *spirit* in a company. I was in Grande Prairie, Alberta, and ready to head home on the 4:15 pm flight. Our flight was delayed five hours due to a problem in a wind-speed detector on the back of the plane. Here is the letter I received:

*Dear Janis,*

On behalf of WestJet, I would like to apologize for the interruption in your travel plans on Wednesday, September 26, 2007. We realize that delays are inconvenient and can potentially affect the rest of your travel itinerary. We acknowledge the delay you experienced while traveling with us, and hope you understand that WestJet will continuously endeavour to bring you the most reliable service offered in the airline industry.

You are a valued guest, and we would like to make it up to you. To thank you for your loyalty, and ask you to fly with WestJet again, we have set up a Future Travel Credit (FTC)* for you in the amount of $84.00 CA. We hope this gesture shows that we are serious about keeping your business. This credit will not only ease the cost of your next trip, but it gives us the opportunity to provide the reliable, friendly and affordable air travel experience that is WestJet.

Thank you for your understanding and patience. If you have any questions or concerns you would like us to address, please feel free to use our Interactive Feedback Corner at www.westjet.com.

*Sincerely,*

*Ken McKenzie*
*Executive Vice-President – Operations*

When was the last time an airline company sent you an apology and a refund from the executive vice-president of the company? I always fly WestJet to wherever they fly!

## SPIRIT DEFINED

Spirit is represented by your attitude.

Attitude is your thoughts, your feelings, your actions.

Your thoughts are yours to choose, and those thoughts create a feeling in you, either positive or negative. As a result, the action you cause because of your thoughts and feelings reflects your attitude.

If you have negative thoughts, you cannot possibly feel good inside. As a result, the Law of Attraction will give you what you are thinking: negative results and a negative attitude.

If, however, your spirit is one of joy, happiness, and positive attitude, then you feel that way and you start to attract great results because of it. Everything is wonderful because of your spirit and positive attitude.

## UNDERSTANDING YOUR SENSES

One of the key elements that I have learned in my coaching of others is that most people are guided only by their five senses.

As a result, their spirit and thinking can be influenced by others. Let me share an example.

Most people read a newspaper every day. Have you seen many positive news stories in the paper? Does it set your spirit and thinking up for a day of attracting joy and passion? No! Any positive news stories are buried in the depths of the articles, and you have to wind your way through the doom and gloom to find them – if they are there at all. So why don't we have positive-news newspapers? They don't sell. Only gossip and fear sell.

By using only your five senses you are at the mercy of other people's opinions just as in reading a paper every day that reports only the negatives. You start to feel negative about what you are reading. You start to believe that our world is falling apart and that you should be afraid of the future. We need to not only use our five senses every day but also to use what are called our intellectual faculties.

Now, most people, when asked what their intellectual faculties are, do not know.

## YOUR INTELLECTUAL FACULTIES

1. Perception

2. Will

3. Imagination

4. Memory

5. Intuition

6. Reason

**Perception** is the way I see something, the way you see something, and the way it really is. Each of us comes with a different perception, and what I have learned over the past years is that things are not always as they seem. Most of our perceptions have been inherited from our families and friends. Because of what I have learned, I do not make quick judgments anymore.

For example, I was driving with a friend of mine, and she noticed an elderly, dirty-clothed man walking down the street. She stated, "Look at that bum – there are more and more needy people living in our area, and it is really scary." I looked and realized that he was our neighbor's dear 90-year-old dad who every day went out to collect cans and bottles to help his granddaughter's school raise money for field trips. Yes, he looked grubby – because he was digging in trash cans and walking through fields looking for his treasures.

Now do you understand perception? I always STOP and THINK before I make any judgment, because more times than not I am totally wrong. What are your perceptions?

The next faculty is **Will**. Will is the ability to concentrate and stay focused on an idea to the exclusion of all other distractions.

Emerson said, "The only thing that can grow is the thing we give energy to."

How do you stay focused to the exclusion of all other distractions?

Let me share an example. Two years ago, Bob Proctor asked me to consider working with his wife in a network marketing company as one way to have multiple streams of income. I wasn't all that excited about the idea, but I decided to do it over a three-month period and then measure how I had done and where I was with my success. I started in late September, and in early October, we had a flood in our home that destroyed all rooms except my office and the bathroom. We had workmen ripping things apart both upstairs and downstairs and leaving us with nothing repaired over a four-month period. During this time, I applied my will, put my head down, and attracted 40 people to come to work with me. By February, the company had paid me an amazing bonus for applying my will and succeeding. I might add that of the people I attracted, some are still on our Mastermind calls three years later.

**Imagination**. We have talked about this extensively in the beginning of the book. This is the magic ingredient that lets you become really clear about what you want.

**Memory**. Do you know that we have a perfect memory? "What?" you say. "No, I don't." That is exactly why you don't. We all go around stating that we have a terrible memory and that we always forget. In other words, we say it and attract that result. I now say that I have a perfect memory, and when I need to remember something I sit down quietly and let the answer come.

The other evening Curt and I were dining out and some patients of Curt's were at the other table. I had helped out in Curt's clinic six years or more ago, and I recognized the lady that came over to say hello. Curt could remember their first names but not their last. As if it were yesterday, I recalled their last name. It is calmness of spirit and knowing that you will remember that lets you do so. Go to www.successtoolbox.com for reference books that will help you improve your memory.

**Intuition** is our sixth sense. I am sure that you have experienced walking into a room and sensing an uneasy feeling. You were aware of a negative vibration or negative energy all around you. Or how about when you have felt deep inside that you need to do something? The thoughts or ideas may have come to you during a quiet moment, and you asked yourself, "Is this the right thing to do or wrong? Good or bad?" But what you need to ask yourself is, **"Will this move me towards my success?"** If it will, DO IT.

One example that I like to share is my intuition about parking spots. I always find a parking spot at the front of the door I am going to. It never fails me. So sure am I about finding a spot that it is now second nature for me, and I don't have to think about it consciously – it is always there.

**Reason** is what sets humans apart from animals – our ability to reason. If you and your pet are in a room together, your pet knows it is in the room, but it doesn't know that it knows it is in the room.

We do, and it is our reason that guides us to understand what we want.

# SPIRIT IS ALWAYS PRESENT

Spirit is 100 percent evenly present at all times. People set up frequencies that are based on their awareness of themselves and the emotions they are experiencing. Where is your spirit? Until you start to think about this and understand where you are, you will not be successful in reaching the big dream you set at the start of this book.

What do you believe in? Have you thought about this, or do you follow what everyone else does without knowing why? Are you positive and at ease, or are you negative and dis-eased, meaning experiencing disease because of your attitude and feelings? Spirit embraces how you treat others and how you give to and receive from others.

What is the spirit in your business? Do you envision yourself and your team having absolutely positive attitudes at all times? How do you contribute to your community? Are you mentoring students, engaging the colleges, or interacting with people who live in your business environment?

Environment should be a global initiative, and the businesses of the future are going to be successful if they focus on this. What byproduct is your business venture producing and affecting the environment and community where you are? How are you and your ideas contributing to the rest of the world? Are you leading with environmental practices just because you believe in them? What city have you chosen to be in? Is it vibrant and leading with values that are in tune with yours? Are you prepared to give to the charities in your community that believe in what you and your spirit believe in?

Ask yourself these questions as part of your strategy, structure, skills, social, and systems within your business venture. Your SPIRIT will shine through in everything you do.

# SPIRIT IN YOUR PERSONAL BEING

Your spirit in your personal life will come from understanding your PURPOSE in life.

This is where your personal being and your entrepreneurial spirit must integrate. In order to understand your values, it is crucial to examine your purpose in life. What do I mean by *purpose*? Why are you on this earth? What purpose are you expected to fulfill?

YOUR PURPOSE

The following is from an exercise that was offered by Nikken at their *Humans Being More* seminar. It is the basis on which each of us must begin to reflect on our purpose in life and business.

*Each individual has a unique purpose. It is important that you uncover your purpose. People only begin to fulfill their creative potential when they have a high degree of alignment in their lives – that is, when their pursuits and conscious goals are in line with their own purpose.*

The most fundamental definition of personal power is having the capacity to realize one's purpose. Personal vision is the key to unlocking its power. Vision is a picture of the future that one wants to create. Vision is the vehicle for bringing purpose into the realm of acts and commitments.

A second key promise regarding personal power is that what an individual holds in his consciousness tends to become real in the external world. The problem is that when people are not in very deep touch with their personal purpose, they pursue objectives in conflict with it. This sets up an inner conflict that limits their power and forces them to become highly manipulative in trying to accomplish their objectives. This is why creative power is released when an individual aligns with his/her personal purpose.

A powerful reinforcing process develops for highly creative persons as they become internally aligned. The results they create in their lives become more consistent with their personal purpose. This leads to deeper understanding of that purpose, clearer vision, more commitment to their vision, and in turn, to deeper alignment and creative capacity.

# MOVING TOWARD VALUES, NEEDS, OR WANTS

Lisa Rigato is a purpose coach, a colleague, and a dear friend. Lisa helps you to identify your eight most important values and takes you through an exercise to help you pinpoint what your true values are and WHY. Boy, can she continue to ask you WHY! She does this because it really encourages you to think about what is meaningful to you, and then she helps you align to your values. She claims that within six forty-five-minute conversations with her over the phone and some homework on your part, you can easily identify your true purpose in life. Visit Lisa at www.daystarvisionsinc.com.

# MY PURPOSE AND MISSION

Your mission statement reflects your personal constitution, set of beliefs, or value system. It addresses questions like the following and helps define how to pursue your goals.

Answer the following questions to assist you in determining what is important to you.

1. What is my life about?

2. What do I value?

3. What do I treasure?

4. What is really important?

5. What do I do in my life that is worthwhile?

*Purpose is to BE*
*Mission is to DO*

Now that you are starting to understand your purpose, let's look at taking this into the entrepreneurial world of business.

# INTEGRATING YOUR PERSONAL PURPOSE INTO YOUR BUSINESS

Building your personal spirit will lead your entrepreneurial spirit. Here are some of the values that come to mind:

- Persistence: never give up; learn as you make mistakes.

- Courage: have the courage to face others who would tell you that it will not work. Use your will to help you focus on your path.

- Honesty and Integrity: say what you mean and mean what you say. Build a positive bank account with others, and you will always have people to help you when you need it.

- Decision: learn to make decisions. Successful people are people who make decisions quickly and seldom change their minds, even if it looks as if they might fail.

Unsuccessful people are unable to make quick decisions and change their minds often, resulting in poor results. Be a decision-maker and people will look to you more and more often as a leader.

- Desire: never lose your desire. Become a motivator and use your imagination to inspire and lead others.

- Education: Indulge in life-long learning that helps you grow, then give it back to others. Recognize that life-long learning can be as effective as formal education.

- Motivation: what inspires you? Clearly knowing your purpose and finding joy as you set out to achieve your purpose in life will give you the motivation necessary to succeed.

- Implementation: this will seem so easy once you understand what this book is giving you. Follow through on what you promise.

- Humor: if you aren't having fun, you are not doing what you should truly be doing. Use humor to encourage, inspire, and motivate others and yourself.

- Meditation: a key ingredient is to sit quietly and contemplate what you desire. In all the research I have done, this is the key to success. Get quiet and get results.

- Affirmation: positively repeating what you want, how great you are, and what a great spirit you have will set up the vibrations that will attract that which you seek.

- Nature: nothing will inspire you as much as being in nature and seeing the magnificently planned patterns of the universe. The quiet alone will awe and inspire you. It will lead to better meditation once you experience it.

- Calmness: as James Allen says:

*"Calmness of mind is one of the beautiful jewels of wisdom. It is the result of long and patient effort in self-control. Its presence is an indication of ripened experience, and of a more than ordinary knowledge of the laws and operations of thought."*

# FINDING YOUR WORD

Let me share with you how I came to implement spirit into my personal and business life. Several people have helped to influence me to concentrate on the spirit I truly desire for myself. My friend Ines Rivas helped me to learn how to meditate, and one day in her living room in San Antonio, Texas, we were meditating together when she clapped her hands to get me to open my eyes and told me that my word was FLOW. I thought, "Okay, my word is flow – now what does that mean?" Well, I started to use this word to plan my day. As I start out in my car, I think of perfect flow in my travels: no traffic problems, calm driving at the speed limit, every light green in front of me, lanes free ahead, and a parking space at the front door of my destination.

What? Are you crazy? I can hear your thoughts now. No, I am not, and my husband Curt so believes in what I believe that he now does the same.

Let me explain through an example of the opposite of what I am telling you here. I left home at 6:50 am on a Thursday to go to downtown Edmonton to run my first leadership class for ATCO Electric. I hit three red lights just down the road from our home, someone almost cut me off on Baseline Road, and as I was turning onto 105 Street another person cut me off. I reached the parking lot, and there wasn't a spot in sight. I got into the hotel, and there wasn't a sign telling me where the training was taking place. THERE WASN'T ANY TRAINING. I WAS A WEEK AHEAD OF MYSELF! The Universe was trying to tell me to turn back! Now, had I paid attention to my intuition sending me messages that I wasn't supposed to go downtown, I would have saved some time and effort.

I have come to trust my word *flow*, and I would ask you to seriously consider a word that will work for you.

Another person who has helped me in finding my spirit is Irene Martina. Irene is an international clairvoyant and speaker, and through her ability to see, she has helped me to take the best possible route in my entrepreneurial journey. Irene helps set your business goals for a six-month period and gives you insight on what and with whom you should be aligning your ideas. Visit Irene at www.irenemartina.com.

I am a firm believer of finding the easiest and most productive tools you can possibly find for your business and personal success. One tool that I have added this past year is a meditation technique from the Centerpointe Research Institute, the brainchild of Bill Harris. The Holosync Solution program has given me a method to mediate in a way I have never been able to before, and the results are amazing. Visit his website at www.centerpointe.com to investigate what he has to offer.

*"Keep away from small people who try to belittle your ambitions. Small people always do that, but the really great make you feel that you, too, can become great."*

**- Mark Twain**

# CHAPTER

## SUCCESS

## CELEBRATING YOUR SUCCESS

The preceding chapters have helped you to focus on key S's and areas to which you must pay attention for your business and personal success. This chapter on success is critical. How do YOU celebrate success? What does success mean to you?

*"Success is the progressive realization of a worthy ideal."*

**- Earl Nightingale**

Earl Nightingale applied this definition to his life for 40 years before he passed away in 1989. He formulated this definition after 17 years of intensive research. It is a definition that I use because it is in harmony with the laws of the universe.

What is your definition of success? Be sure to establish what is meaningful to you, and I believe that you will never find a definition as true as the one above.

If you have your head down, only making money, there is going to be a life to be paid. Remember talking about multiple streams of revenue? Well, success needs to be rounded. It must be reflected in every aspect of your life. Look at your personal life, family, relationships, community, business, spirituality, and health. How are you doing in each area? Are you balanced and prosperous in all of them?

I have chosen to share with you a story of a person who has succeeded and who I believe truly understands the secret to success. Glen is a friend, partner, and entrepreneur. His story will inspire you, and within his story, look for the S's that Glen has successfully blended into his passion for entrepreneurship.

"I can't describe the feeling, but I have always had the entrepreneurial spirit. Even when I was six years old, I was already thinking of ways to make a better product or provide a better service. I knew at the time that I wanted more money, but I hadn't come from a family that was business-oriented, so they couldn't really teach me how to achieve this other than to go to school, get an education, then get a good job. So I depended on myself and where my brain was at the time, and thankfully, my grandfather nurtured this spirit. He often laughed at my ideas, but he would still encourage me to keep going with them. My grandfather was a mentor, even though he was a farmer, not a businessman, and he believed in me.

"When I was in my teens, I started to put some of my ideas into practice. I was always criticized as a dreamer. My family and friends would say, 'Come on, Glen, it has to be reasonable; your ideas are so far-fetched.' Of course, that only made me more convinced that I could pull it off. I didn't know how to go about it, and there wasn't any person to help choose the next entrepreneurial step. However, I had the passion and the desire… nothing more. I didn't have any money or practical knowledge.

"I started by getting into the little Bobcat business in the mid-70s when industry was only beginning to use Bobcats to do landscaping. Well, it skyrocketed, and I could hardly keep up. It was my first entrance into business and I loved it. My dad purchased the Bobcat, and I leased it from him. As you can see, by this time my parents were beginning to replace my grandfather's support with their own.

"During the summer, as I was attending university to be a teacher, I worked on the oil rigs a lot. For several consecutive years, actually starting at the age of fifteen, I missed Christmas and Easter holidays at home so I could make double time working on the rigs. By this time, I was dedicated to making lots of money so that I could go to university and become a teacher.

"Now, as I worked on the oil rigs, working nights with lots of snow and cold, I became convinced that this was what *I didn't want* to do, and I remember reminding myself repeatedly, 'I will have succeeded somewhere in my life when I am able to hire one of these rigs to drill my own well.'

"So you could say that I had identified my success. I was going to either own one of these rigs or I was going to take it one step further and become that oil company that hired the rig and its workers to work for me. That was why all the riggers were there, right? To make money for the oil company! Why not instead become one of them? I was able to put it all in proper context, and I think that was very important. Most people never do that; they continue to work for the company never realizing that they could be the company. You need to ask yourself: where do you fit in the scheme of things? What are you doing? Where are you in the pecking order? Where do you really want to be? When I used to share that with the other guys on the rigs, they would mostly mock me. But you know what? I did drill wells, many of them – many were dusters, some of them not!

"Achieving this was my epitome of succeeding as an entrepreneur!

"Now, I can honestly say that through my whole life I wasn't so much starting these different businesses for the money. It was to succeed, to show people and myself that I could succeed and that I could make it work. Maybe it was because I grew up in a family that didn't understand the entrepreneurial spirit. I had the innate need to succeed, and initially those close to me would wonder where my ideas came from.

"Wasn't it good enough to have become a teacher? So why not teach? My wife thought she married a teacher, but I fooled her.

"Let me explain the basics of being an entrepreneur. Firstly, an entrepreneur is probably not aware that he/she is one, except for the inexplicable fire that burns inside him/her, the desire for more out of life than what his/her present role is offering. It will smolder if you don't fuel this spirit; personal contentment will often seem just out of reach if you don't follow this urge. Secondly, you must get to a point in your life where you need to identify this urge and act.

"Can you become an entrepreneur? Well, I believe there is a learned process, but I'm not sure you would have the same success that a natural entrepreneur would have. I don't think you can teach passion, which is critical to the entrepreneur's spirit. In order to be successful, you have to be passionate in what you do. Passion is the cornerstone to entrepreneurial success.

"How would I define the actions of an entrepreneur? Even without resources, you have to be flexible and willing to change direction quickly in business. There are definitely failures along the way, and the most defining moment for me was the moment when I began to recognize failure for what it was and simply proceeded in another direction. Sometimes it means cutting your losses and going on with another project, but other times it means implementing another plan.

"Let me share with you that moment. It was such a stressful event, emotionally and spiritually, because I felt I let myself, my family, and God down. A business deal works because I put my heart and soul into it. But for whatever reason, when I get to the precipice or the edge of the cliff and I look over… I see darkness; and the depth to which I am about to fall. I realized that day that I had to turn around and go in the other direction. This happened sometime in the wee hours of the morning in Medicine Hat, Alberta. I was responsible for almost losing a commercial bingo hall after having convinced my wife to relocate our family from one side of the province to the other to take this business on. Along with a friend, we had all of our equity at stake – we were about to lose everything. I had been up for several nights writing out alternative scenarios for survival. Unaware of what I was learning at the time, I was in fact experiencing how to create contingency plans. The flexibility that I referred to earlier was now being implemented. Today I don't need to sit down and write it out; I can do it entirely in my mind. I am constantly doing it as I go through my day.

"A business venture will kick out a bad result, and I will automatically begin the process of building a contingency plan. If someone says something to me that puts me on red alert, I'm automatically going into contingency mode. I think that is what allows me to have reasonably good success in business. I am very good at this process, and I didn't know what it was until a few years ago, when my wife asked me what I was thinking about, and it occurred to me that I was formulating another contingency plan. I am always in planning mode. I go through the process and visualize what I need to do.

"Visualization is extremely important. You must define what you want, and it takes nothing more than a creative mind and the ability to look up at the blank wall and see the answer anywhere you are without the painful experience of always putting it on paper. You have to practice this.

"Intuition is an innate part of you. Can you hone it? No doubt about it! When in doubt about a decision, let your intuition guide you. It sure has served me well.

"You must abide by two things as an entrepreneur. Separate entrepreneurship from business. Business demands good stewardship. It has already been invented, most likely by entrepreneurs. Entrepreneurship is creating and changing systems – I consider that to be a good entrepreneur.

"Follow two fundamental principles to guide your business journeys: having passion and overcoming the fear of failure. Recognize failure for what it is and go the other way. How do I know what direction to go?

"I use a simple formula: identify the break-even in every business, which surprisingly most people don't want to identify. I suppose they don't want the outcome to dictate their decision to proceed or not with their venture – again I can only assume that they are caught up in the fervor of their business concept. The concept might be great, but you must consider its potential profitability. You cannot be personal, sentimental, or emotional about it. What is the break-even? Write down costs. Predict the revenues – this is the fun part. Have due diligence, ask people, and read relevant materials. After you have completed this process, return and do it again with a critical mind. If it is a winner, you should be able to teach your spouse or friend everything there is know about the venture.

"I pride myself on not always having the answers but on always knowing who to ask. I always hire the best brains available. Don't skimp on professional advice. They are usually smarter than we are.

"When I first started, I did not know the advice that I have given you, but what kept me going was my passion and intuition. That's what kept me going. Honest to God, was I fearful? You're damn right! I was scared every month I didn't have a regular paycheck to bring home. I would sometimes work for a couple of years building a profitable business only to sell it for a meaningful paycheck. This was wrong. Try not to sell positive cash flow; borrow against this cash flow instead.

"Who do I admire? Warren Buffet. He is one of the most brilliant entrepreneurs and academic business minds in the world. His ability to determine intrinsic values better then anyone else is paramount. In many ways, he has simply gone into the business world, uncovered some of the best entrepreneurs, and bought them with the purchase of their companies. I believe that is what he has done. Warren Buffet is now the epitome of that final frontier of entrepreneurship. He has challenged the business world and has won the challenge. His reward has been wealth – massive amounts of it. In an about-turn, he has returned this reward by wishing that it be redistributed to those less fortunate. He has won the entrepreneurial game.

"As I have stated, at the beginning of my journey, I needed to depend solely on my passion and intuition to guide me. Now that I have gained some success, I've come to rely on other people's skills more. I don't worry so much about the break-even points; I let others do that for me. I depend on these people for the planning, financing, and marketing of a project as well. Experience has also helped hone my decision-making ability. Blending the facts and recommendations of management, I can usually arrive at a conclusion more efficiently than I once did.

"I value my ability to put together teams, and if I am blessed to continue to succeed as an entrepreneur, I hope to create wealth for this management team as well.

"During the years, I didn't do it for the money. Now, don't get me wrong, I wanted to provide for my family. But I didn't worry about the money. I always knew money would come in behind me if I provided a better service or a better product than the next guy. Hire people who want to do the same. Obviously they need a skill set of some sort, but given that, choose confident and passionate people for your business teams. If they are bright and willing, one should be able to teach them what they don't know.

"Currently, I participate in the ownership of some fifteen private companies with a team of very competent management. I consider myself the coach, the support system, and the cheerleader. I want others to succeed; I include them in the profits as well as try to incorporate them as partners. I've had some lousy partners in the past, and I have learned to live by an old adage when picking partners: those who do not trust may not be trusted. Legal agreements are a prerequisite, but trust should still be considered the pillars of any business partnership. Strive for it.

"How do I find my balance? I am still experimenting with that. I am trying to spend some time in the South during the winter months working on my golfing habit, to spend summers on the farm enjoying its pace, and to allow some business mixed in between. This transition is difficult for entrepreneurs because their passion has most likely afflicted them with a business addiction. The years of deal-making provide one with a natural chemical rush which I fear has been very addictive. Maybe the solution will be the Twelve Steps! I don't know, but I am trying to find it. Developing my spirituality has helped and has become very important to me. There has to be meaning in what you are doing. Get to the top and give it all back."

You will recognize in Glen's story that he has applied the S's we have covered so far in this book. Now let me add to Glen's story. Glen began to gradually lose his hearing over a period of ten years. It was a traumatic and hard experience for Glen and his family. Despite this hearing loss and a cochlear implant to allow him to improve his hearing again in 2000, Glen never let his handicap get in his way. He learned to lip-read, he learned to carry extra batteries with him, and in noisy crowds Glen goes back to lip-reading. Never once did Glen let this handicap interfere with what he knew he could do. Now he admits he uses his loss of hearing as a benefit for him. When he really needs to think and concentrate he turns his implant off, and the world and distractions go away.

## WHAT IS YOUR HANDICAP?

If you are a golfer, you will truly understand what a handicap is; the lower the handicap, the better a golfer you are. Well, there are entrepreneurs and would-be entrepreneurs who do have physical handicaps who have risen above them and are functioning perfectly in their business and personal lives.

There are also handicaps that are produced by you and your thinking.

Ask yourself, "What handicap do I have that is stopping me from succeeding? Is it fear, is it the opinion of others, is it lack of funds?" Whatever you can conceive, it might be your handicap. Napoleon Hill talks about the importance of desire but he also states that you need to have the undying faith that what you want will happen.

My husband and I were driving in a snow storm this past winter, and we were not able to put on our high beams to see better because of the intensity of the snow. It made me realize that as long as we could see in front of us, the next section of the road would be illuminated as we needed it. It is this type of faith that you need to think about every day. Let the Universe light the next step for you and count on your intuition to realize that it is the right path to follow.

Don't let handicaps stop you. Identify what is holding you back and deal with it. Face it like Glen has and develop a contingency plan to correct it.

For ideas on techniques to overcome handicaps, go to www.successtoolbox.com.

## CELEBRATING SUCCESS

How do you celebrate success? Do you? Many people go through life working and gaining money, but they forget to celebrate.

What is success for you? It should be a balance between work and home – possibly a great relationship, health, or wealth. Only you know what success represents for you.

One key technique that I have applied consistently over the years is business journaling. What is this? Well, it means keeping track of all your successes. As humans, we tend to remember only the things that didn't go well. This record helps you to see what you have accomplished and thus gives you the opportunity to celebrate all that has been accomplished. It helps to create a compelling future for yourself and others who are on the journey with you.

How do you record your successes?

Go to www.successtoolbox.com to receive your free e-business journal.

*Janis Celebrating Your Success*

# PERSONAL SUCCESS

Spend some time here thinking about your health. Without it, nothing else matters. I can tell you so many stories about friends whom we have lost who spent all their time collecting money and then died because they didn't take the time for themselves or their family. These are people who amassed fortunes, became sick, and then found that they couldn't buy their health back. If they did, their lifestyle was certainly compromised.

The key word here is HABIT. I have recently really come to recognize how important this is. We all hear about the habit of exercise, the habit of eating healthy food, and the habit of taking care of ourselves. Well, for some reason, four years ago, after an injury to my left leg and knee on the tennis court, I stopped exercising. Previously, I had always been a fit person, exercising, lifting weights, and playing sports. Suddenly, I stopped. I had surgery on my knee and just stopped doing anything. The habit that I had so treasured just disappeared. Needless to say, I gained weight and lost body tone. This year I decided to start again. It started with a decision in my conscious mind; then, I allowed my sub-conscious to align with it. This created the vibrations in my body that helped me find some integrated tools that would help me to stick to my decision. I found a machine that I could work out on daily for 10 minutes a day, and for 20 days I set the habit. Then I added two other health tools, massage every two weeks and a yoga class once a week – this almost killed me, but again I set a habit outside of my home. I am astounded at the results. Now I am eating healthy foods to accentuate the results. Habit is the key to maintaining your health, and the results will show by boosting your entrepreneurial energy.

So, personal success to me is LEARNING and applying the art of discipline, relaxation, meditation, and getting in touch with nature and the Universe. Build a habit and have some FUN. Become a child again and learn and just enjoy the moment. Enjoy your family, enjoy your friends, take time to be yourself, and let the entrepreneurial spirit guide you to a better, balanced you. Become passionate about YOU.

On any flight today, the flight crew will tell you, "In the event of a change in air pressure, the oxygen mask will come down from the panel above. If you are traveling with small children or others needing help, PUT THE OXYGEN MASK ON YOURSELF FIRST."

Celebrating your success means putting yourself first; find time for you and take care of yourself. Then celebrate and take others with you.

*"Learn to enjoy every minute of your life. Be happy now. Don't wait for something outside of yourself to make you happy in the future. Think how really precious is the time you have to spend, whether it's at work or with your family."*

**- Earl Nightingale**

# CHAPTER

---

# SHARING

*"Make sharing a magnificent obsession."* My friend and colleague, Colin Markin, called me one day with this great quote. Every person needs to make this a cornerstone to their success.

So we have looked at success and how you want to celebrate, and now I want to talk about sharing your success with others. Whether it is wealth, kindness, mentoring, and/or supporting, sharing is what brings you even more success, both personally and business-wise. You must realize that money is intended to be circulated; you cannot hoard it or you will stop it from coming toward you. For this reason, sharing is one of the crucial lessons to be learned for your success.

I want to share with you two concepts that I have purposely saved to the end of the book. You have read and learned about the tools necessary to help you step out and become an entrepreneur. Now I want you to concentrate on what you are thinking and feeling as you do so.

The first concept is one that Bob Proctor uses as the basis of all his programs. As a LifeSuccess Consultant with Bob I have drawn this concept hundreds of times for anyone that is willing to learn from it. It is the basis of my success and has led me to explore further to understand how it works. It is called the *Stickperson*.

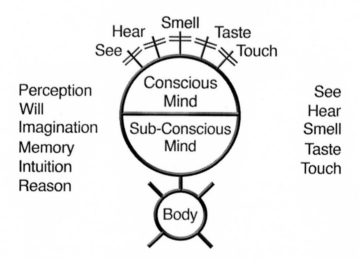

The Stickperson was developed by Dr. Thruman Fleet from San Antonio, Texas, in the 1930s. He was working in the Health Sciences. What his stickperson depicts is a picture of your mind.

When I ask people to explain what their mind looks like, they often describe their brain, or something like fog and confusion. Why do we need a picture of the mind? We think in pictures. If I ask you to think of a feather, you are able to see a feather flash across the screen of your mind. Now picture the home that you live in. There it is flashing across the screen of your mind: your home.

Since our mind is the unseen part of our personality, we must use our imagination to build an image – and this can be accomplished with the Stickperson. At the beginning of this book I had you concentrate on imagining the perfect business and personal life. Now let's take it a step further.

Look at the picture on page 164. The large circle represents our mind and the smaller circle represents our body. The mind is proportionally larger than the body because our mind creates everything. Our body is a manifestation from the mind. We only live in a body, but the mind is our control centre and exists in every cell of our body. Consider, however, how we spend most of our time looking only at the body in our physical world, but we do not put any effort into focusing on the creator of all these things… our mind.

Mind is made up of two parts, your conscious mind at the top of the large circle and the sub-conscious mind at the lower part.

The conscious mind deals with thought. Our conscious mind can choose. It can accept, reject, or neglect any idea. It has the ability to make choices. The conscious mind is your thinking mind.

Now let's look at the subconscious, or lower part of the large circle. The subconscious mind cannot choose; IT CAN ONLY ACCEPT. It does not know the difference between good or evil, big or small, black or white. It cannot differentiate between that which is real or imagined. It only knows that when you choose a thought in your conscious mind, it has to accept it. Your subconscious reflects the thoughts you choose in your conscious mind. It is the storehouse of all our memories, habits, conditioning beliefs, and our self image. The subconscious is your feeling mind.

Your attitude controls the quality of everything in your life. Remember I talked about attitude as your thoughts, your feelings and your results? Your thoughts (conscious mind) cause your feelings (sub-conscious mind) and your feelings are expressed in actions (vibrations in body) and your actions produce your results. That which we think about, we become, and our results reflect what we have been thinking about. That is why I have asked you to be clear about what you want in business and personal life. So if you want to change your results, then you must change what you are thinking about.

On the days that you are sitting around with an attitude of "I don't want to" the Stickperson will help you to remember that you need to change your thoughts to positive winning thoughts and a winning attitude.

In the chapter on Spirit, I explain the five senses and how we allow other people's opinions to affect our thoughts. The antennae at the top of the large circle in the graph represent these five senses bringing us information from everywhere. Remember our conscious mind can choose the thoughts we want. You were given the ability to consciously and deliberately think anything you want to. Ask yourself "What am I thinking?" Which thoughts are mine and which are not?

The key is to become emotionally involved with your thoughts.

The graph also shows you the intellectual faculties that I have covered in the chapter on Spirit. This is the better way for us to influence our thinking, rather than relying on our physical senses. It is the higher side of our nature, our intellect, that is found within these faculties.

| Perception | Will | Imagination |
|------------|------|-------------|
| Memory | Intuition | Reason |

Go back to the Spirit chapter and review these faculties again. Our intellectual faculties are like mental muscles, they must be used in order for them to develop and become strong. When we allow these faculties to govern our thoughts we create an intellectual mind that allows us to really think. They are the keys to success and they are the areas that you need to work on to continue to achieve success.

The last concept that I wish to share with you is through the discovery of Esther and Jerry Hicks and *The Teachings of Abraham*. One of their books, *The Astonishing Power of Emotions,* supports the Stickperson and the need to get emotionally involved with your thoughts. Jerry asks you, "What if someone told you that the true measure of your success in life is your joy?" Their latest book, *Money and The Law of Attraction*, will help you to understand how to tell your story to attract what you desire.

It is this thinking from these books that has led me to understand true success.

Esther and Jerry's books help you to understand how to change your thinking through better use of words and to ask yourself, "What feelings am I experiencing and why?" They have given me a tool to ensure my thoughts, feelings and actions – my attitude – is one of joy and harmony. Visit them at www.abraham-hicks.com.

## SHARING BECOMES YOUR PASSION

Now begins your journey to share with others. It might be money, it might be stories, it might be a legacy – but you must give back.

Become a mentor to others. Identify what you want to share and with whom who you want to share it. Is it your community, a cause, your church, your family, friends, or colleagues? Decide how you are going to do this.

Find a mentor whom you admire and support that person's direction. Learn from them, as I did with Bob Proctor, and then pass on the learning to others. My Mastermind group was an obvious opportunity to share what I had learned and to learn from others as well.

Network with others and share your knowledge.

Join or start a Mastermind and share your ideas and support with other like-minded people.

Help others learn, and give them the opportunity to follow your lead in success. There is no better feeling than when you see someone grow and prosper from your learning.

Walk the talk. You have to express what you believe. People are watching you, and they will quickly understand that you do not believe what you speak if you do not show it every day.

Ask yourself: what is important to you? Is it family, friends, community, spirituality, or something else?

Look at some of the key people in our society today, people who are giving back: Oprah Winfrey, Warren Buffet, Bill Gates, Mary Kay Ash, Anita Roddick.

Oprah Winfrey is one person who epitomizes giving back. Look at the lives she has touched and the initiative she has taken in Africa to help young girls receive an education and become a part of a solution for their nation. She doesn't have to stay on television – she does it for the betterment of others, in order to share and show people that there is a better way. She knows about walking the talk; she lives it every day.

Warren Buffet is someone whom I have not closely followed, but since interviewing Glen, I am reading a book entitled *Buffetology* and learning about his success story. I am realizing that Warren Buffet is giving significantly back to society.

Bill Gates and his wife are leading a campaign and donating money to help American schools become better at educating children.

Mark Kay Ash, founder of Mary Kay Cosmetics, is offering women a chance to truly succeed in network marketing, encouraging, leading, and coaching women to become all they can, and being financially rewarded for doing so.

Anita Roddick founded The Body Shop, a company that has been built on values. These values include not using animals to test their products on and considering the environment in the choices they make for their products. Though Anita is now deceased, people are still lining up to work for The Body Shop.

I am sure you know someone whom you admire who is giving back and building a spirit of oneness with the world. Who can you look up to and emulate for your success?

I want to mention here that asking some of these people to help you is absolutely an option. Don't be afraid to try to connect with someone you admire. There are really big-hearted, successful people who are willing to mentor others. **Don't forget to be one yourself.**

Giving has to be our goal. If you think you can take it with you, guess again. The more money you are willing to send out to the Universe, the more will be coming your way.

Start to imagine how you are going to share your wealth with others. What does it feel like? What are you doing? Who are you giving to?

This will seem so real that you will actually believe you are doing it.

**Here is an example:**

*I am so happy and grateful now that I have attracted $10,000,000. I have hired a jet from Greg Durant of Blue Skies in New York to fly me to Ontario. I have planned a surprise party, by invitation only, at the best hotel in London, Ontario. Every member of my family has received a mysterious invitation to join a benefactor at this hotel. As they arrive, there are flowers, harps playing, and appetizers being served. Curt and I surprise them by walking into the room. Champagne is served, and I call each member of my family up and hand them envelopes. Every person opens their envelope and is shocked by the amount of money on the check. We celebrate all night. The next day, Greg flies us to Alberta, and we invite every member of Curt's family to a similar dinner. We* *again present each of the kids with a check. I write a check for $100,000 to the Lois Hole Hospital for Women and I know that Curt and I are going to help so many women as they are helped in this facility. I call my Mastermind partners and tell them that Greg is going to pick each of them up and that we are meeting in Hawaii in our dream home on the ocean. We are sitting around the magnificent infinity pool, and we are thanking God and the Universe for the opportunity to be together and to read and study as a group.*

## DO YOU GET THE PICTURE?

This is so real to me that I already know I own the money and that I have helped every single person in Curt's and my families and the community, for which I am so grateful. I thank God every day for this.

What is most important here is the word *grateful*. That is why Bob Proctor always starts his Goal Card with, "I am so happy and grateful that…"

Wallace D. Wattles wrote an entire chapter on gratitude in his book *The Science of Getting Rich*.

*"The grateful mind is constantly fixed upon the best. Therefore, it tends to become the best; it takes the form or character of the best and will receive the best… It is necessary, then, to cultivate the habit of being grateful for every good thing that comes to you — to give thanks continuously."*

Most importantly, you must share with yourself. Begin to understand who you truly are inside. If you need some help, get to work and find a coach or mentor to help you realize what you need to do to be fulfilled.

Feel joy in what you do. Take up a hobby and start to soar. What really turns your crank? Find it and take time to enjoy what you are attracting. The more you relax, the more you will attract. Worry, fear, and doubt slide off because you are centered in your universe, and your attitude and celebration of success will guide you to the next place. Napoleon Hill tells us that we don't have to know the how of something – we simply need the next step lit up for us. We have to Let Go and Let God.

## *Enjoy the journey.*

*"...There's such a thing as trying too hard.*
*You've got to sing like you don't need the money...*
*Love like you'll never get hurt...*
*You've got to dance like nobody's watching...*
*It's got to come from the heart if you want it to work."*

**– Kathy Mattea,**
*Come From the Heart*

# BOOKS THE AUTHOR RECOMMENDS

*You2*, Price Pritchett

*Think and Grow Rich*, Napoleon Hill

*The E-Myth*, Michael Gerber

*Wealth Beyond Reason*, Bob Doyle

*Four Hour Work Week*, Timothy Ferriss

*The Science of Getting Rich*, Wallace Wattles

*The Millionaire Mindset*, Gerry Robert

*The Law of Attraction*, Esther and Jerry Hicks

*Ask and It Is Given*, Esther and Jerry Hicks

*The Amazing Power of Deliberate Intent*, Esther and Jerry Hicks

*The Astonishing Power of Emotions*, Esther and Jerry Hicks

*Money and The Law of Attraction*, Esther and Jerry Hicks

*As You Wish*, Carol Gates and Tina Shearon

*As A Man Thinketh*, James Allen

*Spiritual Marketing*, Joe Vitale

*Working With the Law*, Raymond Holliwell

*Being the Best You Can Be in MLM*, John Kalench

# IF YOU ARE INTERESTED IN...

**Coaching** – Janis offers Internet and personal training in:

- The Winner's Image

- The Goal Achiever

- Success Puzzle

- You Were Born Rich

- Purpose Coaching in conjunction with Lisa Rigato, Daystar Visions Inc.

**Speaking** – Janis tailors her speaking sessions to inspire and teach about:

- Law of Attraction

- Making Change Easy

- Energy – Attraction – Results

- Inspiration to Soar

- The Stickperson - Thinking About What You Are Thinking

- Applying Napoleon Hill's Strategies

**Leadership and Sales** – Janis, working with Achieve Global Canada, offers:

- Leadership for Results

- Genuine Leadership

- Professional Selling Skills

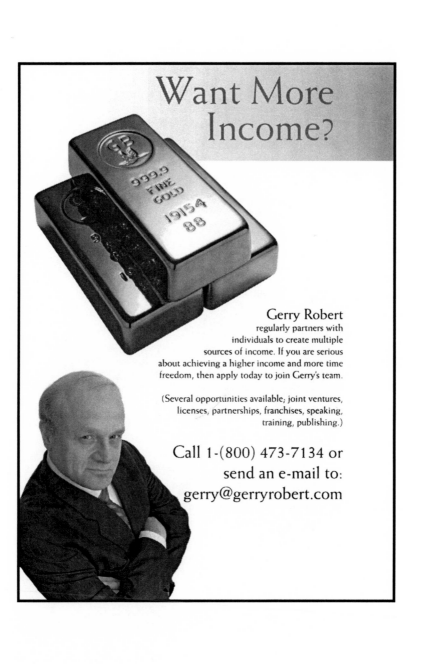

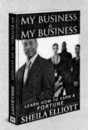
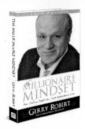

# OTHER BOOKS FROM LIFESUCCESS PUBLISHING

### STOP SINGING THE BLUES

10 powerful strategies for hitting the high notes in your life

**Dr. Cynthia Barnett**
ISBN 978-1-59930-022-1

### DON'T BE A VICTIM! PROTECT YOURSELF

Everything seniors need to know to avoid being taken financially

**Jean Ann Dorrell**
ISBN 978-1-59930-024-5

### A "HAND UP," NOT A "HAND OUT"

The best ways to help others help themselves

**David Butler**
ISBN 978-1-59930-071-9

### A CLIMATE FOR CHANGE

How to ride the wave of change into the 21st century

**Di Worrall**
ISBN 978-1-59930-123-5

### I BELIEVE IN ME

7 ways for woman to step ahead in confidence

**Lisa Gorman**
ISBN 978-1-59930-069-6

### THE COLOR OF SUCCESS

Why color matters in your life, your love, your lexus

**Mary Ellen Lapp**
ISBN 978-1-59930-078-8

### IF NOT NOW, WHEN?

What's your dream?

**Cindy Nielsen**
ISBN 978-1-59930-073-3

### THE SKILLS TO PAY THE BILLS... AND THEN SOME!

How to inspire everyone in your organisation into high performance!

**Buki Mosaku**
ISBN 978-1-59930-058-0

# OTHER BOOKS FROM LIFESUCCESS PUBLISHING

## FROM WAGS TO RICHES

For the secrets to attracting success in your life. Just listen to you dog

**Kim Kapes**
ISBN 978-1-59930-128-0

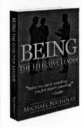

## BEING THE EFFECTIVE LEADER

"Before you can do something You first must be something"

**Michael Nicholas**
ISBN 978-1-59930-093-1

## ATTRACTING FREEDOM

Lifestyle, not life sentence

**Isha Knill**
ISBN 978-1-59930-129-7

## THINK PROPERTY AND GROW RICH

Master buying Australian investment properties in changing times like the experts do

**Melainie White**
ISBN 978-1-59930-167-9

## JOURNEY TO JOY

A womans guide to balancing it all

**Leanne Hawkes-Sobeck**
ISBN 978-1-59930-121-1

## THE SCIENCE OF A PERFECT WEIGHT

A new way of thinking, eating and living to achieve your perfect weight

**Bob Proctor and Melonie Dodaro**
ISBN 978-1-59930172-3

## WINGS OF CHANGE

Discover a new formation to success

**Jim and Katharina Murdoch**
ISBN 978-1-59930-194-5

## BREAKTHROUGH 2 BALANCE

Your journey to emotional freedom

**Alex Reed**
ISBN 978-1-59930-127-3-

# OTHER BOOKS FROM LIFESUCCESS PUBLISHING

## WEALTH MAGNETZ

Your A to Z guide
for abundant living

**Regina
Richardson**
ISBN 978-1-59930-197-6

## BE
## DO
## HAVE

"Create Your Life With
The Law Of Attraction"

**Nicholas Tutora**
ISBN 978-1-59930-213-3

## COMMITMENT TO CHARACTER

Achieving Success
from the Inside Out

**Jean
Watterson**
ISBN 978-1-59930-180-8

## CHANGE YOUR BODY WITH THE WORLDS FITTEST COUPLE

The secret to a
great body revealed

**Matt Thom &
Monica Wright**
ISBN 978-1-59930-065-8

## MORE MONEY THAN MONTH

Stop stressing over
your finances and take
control of your life

**Todd Dean**
ISBN 978-1-59930-256-0

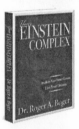

## THE EINSTEIN COMPLEX

Awaken your
inner genius
live your dreams

**Dr. Roger A. Boger**
ISBN 978-1-59930-269-0

## THE EXIT STRATEGY

How to ensure
your success
after the military

**Benjamin Smith**
ISBN 978-1-59930-112-9

## THE IMAGE DOCTOR

Introducing the incredibly
simple orangecard
The ultimate tool for
love, health, career and
financial success!

**Dr. Tory M. Robson**
ISBN 978-1-59930-261-4